NOBODY IS SMARTER THAN EVERYBODY:

"Rod Collins is the living definition of perspicacious—a keen visionary and scribe peering into the future of organizations and telling
the rest of us what we need to know about it. In an age when change
occurs faster than the ability of people to absorb it, the fossilized
bureaucratic business model faces obsolescence. Collins makes a
compelling case, with real-world examples, for organizations to
navigate the continuous whitewater of the Digital Age using the
powerful twin oars of self-management and networked intelligence."

–Doug Kirkpatrick, author of *The No Limits Enterprise:*
Organizational Self-Management in the New World of Work

"My work with owners and executives had included the counsel that
the old model of top-down leadership was perhaps appropriate when
change was measured and slow. In a time of rapid change for individuals, families, and organizations, that model is beyond outdated
to be anti-survival. Rod Collins is a solid thinker who goes beyond
being a theorist—he's "been there and done that" as a C-suite veteran. What he's captured here is a handbook for me and others who
know that the chaos created by rapid change is only beginning. The
winners will figure out how to navigate the new reality, and this book
is a needed and wanted map to the territory."

–Robert White, bestselling author and
world-recognized executive coach

"Power as force and the use of hierarchies to enable it is centuries old.
Power as energy to be shared and cultivated in networks to achieve
extraordinary results is a vastly new and different way of thinking
and acting. In his new book, *Nobody Is Smarter Than Everybody*, Rod
Collins describes in detail the working dynamics of power as energy
manifest in self-managed peer-to-peer networks. Collins shares the

tools and practices peers in networks use to solve problems, organize work, and accomplish results. This book is a must-read for everyone in any organization who recognizes the need to think and act differently is long overdue."

–Larry Cooper, Chief Strategy Officer,
The Hive Professional Network

"In a world of exploding change, organizations need new models for doing business that help them adapt to a quickly evolving landscape while staying true to the values most important to them. Rod Collins' new book *Nobody Is Smarter Than Everybody* has important answers. As we seek new ways of organizing, this book includes solid case studies and concrete tools for leadership in the 21st century."

–Alicia Korten, CEO of The Culture Company

"*Nobody Is Smarter Than Everybody* is a must-read for those seeking a roadmap to collaborative success in today's dynamic work landscape. I found the book to be empowering and insightful. Rod Collins skillfully navigates through real-world examples, illustrating how self-managed peer-to-peer teams foster a culture where teams take ownership of their decisions. This book equips its readers not only with knowledge but with the tools to cultivate a new organizational paradigm where leadership and decision-making are exercised by teams rather than individuals, ultimately making better decisions. I now have a better understanding of how leveraging the collective intelligence of all team members (rather than traditional hierarchies) can combine the strengths of different perspectives into innovative thinking. This book will become your go-to for practical guidance and a companion for those leaders looking to transform to self-managed teams."

–Andrea Szigeth, founder & CEO,
Academy for Institutional Investors, LLC.

"Nobody Is Smarter Than Everybody emerges as a crucial guide to leaders and executives in organizations of all sizes. This book not only explains the "how" and "why" but also provides practical insights and examples. Collins' methods have profoundly influenced my approach to Personal Agility, particularly in how to create alignment among stakeholders so they can make decisions that stick. His approach has been instrumental in several successful engagements. Offering an enlightening and empowering perspective on leadership, this book is a must-read for any leader seeking to navigate the complexities of modern organizational dynamics. Collins's approach, deeply resonant and practically grounded, is a beacon for transformative leadership."

–Peter Stevens, author of *Personal Agility: Unlocking Purpose, Alignment, and Transformation*

"Once you've read *Nobody Is Smarter Than Everybody*, you will view the business world through a different lens—you won't be able to look back and comfortably accept the business models predominantly used today. Every leader driven to success through collective intelligence vs. power and authority will find this book fascinating as well as instructive. This book and Rod's other writings are essential to any leadership education and training for the future."

–Sue Bingham, Founder and Principal, HPWP Consulting Group

"*Nobody Is Smarter Than Everybody* couldn't be a more timely and important contribution to organizational leadership. Rod Collins' latest contribution makes a convincing case that the forces of technological change have made our traditional, hierarchical organizational designs obsolete and that the enduring organizations of the future will distribute decision-making broadly to capture the full power of collective intelligence and insight. If you care about your organization's future, this is a must-read."

–Jim Parker, nationally recognized healthcare leader and founder of JTP Advisors

"I first met Rod Collins some years ago when we collaborated on a training program to teach the leadership principles that create innovative, resilient, agile, and adaptive cultures. During that experience, I learned more from Rod about how to thrive in rapidly changing, uncertain environments than from any other experiences, reading, and training that I have had. *Nobody is Smarter Than Everybody* encapsulates everything that Rod has learned and taught and does so using concrete, credible, consumable examples. This book describes principles that work—and not just in rapidly changing, uncertain environments. I have used the principles that Rod teaches and changed the trajectory of my career and the results of my leadership. Whether someone is new to leadership, recognizes the need to change their approach to leadership, or just needs to be reminded about effective leadership, this book is for them."

–Niel Nickolaisen, director of Enterprise Systems and Security, Utah State University

"Discover a paradigm shift in management thinking with Rod Collins, a trailblazing visionary in the realm of work transformation. His seminal insights on self-management and collective intelligence drive innovation in organizations worldwide. In this book, Rod makes the irrefutable case that our current top-down, hierarchal management structures are incapable of adapting to the current pace of change. He argues that operational efficiency is no longer sufficient to maintain the status quo and that innovation is now table stakes to adapt to our rapidly changing world. This book examines the history, the problems, and, more importantly, the solutions vetted over decades in some of the world's most recognizable brands. He blueprints the working dynamics of non-coercive, self-managed peer-to-peer networks and details the difference between an operational style and an operational system. I strongly recommend this book for executives and business owners seeking to thrive in our rapidly evolving world."

–Bill Sanders, principal and managing director, Roebling Strauss, Inc.

"When Rod talks, people stop and take notes. When he writes, he is the leading edge of innovation in management. This book is the perfect extension of all his work. Insightful, timely, and usable. If you're looking for a new edge in management thinking and you need to prepare your team for the coming challenges of the next decade, this is your book. Apply it immediately. Highly recommended."

—Bill Beausay, coauthor of *True Greatness: Mastering the Inner Game of Business Success*

"Rod Collins has done it again. In *Nobody Is Smarter Than Everybody*, he parses out the nuances that characterize adaptive companies from those fixed in traditional thinking. He then provides a clear, logical basis for adapting thinking that retains familiar elements of the past while laying out the challenge for leaders who rely on authority over collective intelligence. An essential read for the many executives whose role is more complex and on the edge than they are aware of."

—Dawna Jones, host of the *Inspirational Insights* podcast

"Rod makes a compelling case for replacing traditional command and control hierarchies with more nimble and effective self-managed teams. His insights provide a roadmap for how businesses can succeed in a world where collective knowledge and distributed authority is the only way to keep pace."

—Michael Fazio, Director of Strategy at Jump Associates

Nobody Is Smarter Than Everybody

Rod Collins

To my wife, Glenda
for being the surprise and delight of my life

Table of Contents

1

A RADICALLY DIFFERENT WORLD

L et's begin with a thought experiment. Imagine you step into a time machine. Your destination is to travel back to central Pennsylvania in the early 1700s. The trip begins smoothly enough. However, along the way back in time, you suddenly encounter the most severe turbulence you've ever experienced. After some very terrifying moments, the vehicle somehow manages to arrive on the gentle slopes of the early eighteenth-century commonwealth.

As you breathe a sigh of relief, thanking your lucky stars that you are still alive, the captain tells you that she has good news and bad news. The good news is that despite the time machine's obvious malfunction, you have arrived safely. The bad news is, because you are three hundred years in the past, you don't have the technology to repair the vehicle. So, the captain regretfully announces that you and your fellow passengers are all now permanent residents of this eighteenth-century agricultural paradise.

As you sit there stunned, thinking that this is not the trip you signed up for and contemplating how you will adjust to spending the rest of your life in the eighteenth century, you are suddenly alarmed by a very troubling thought: How easy will it be for you to find work in your current profession? In the Agrarian Age, there were not many executives, managers, analysts, or technical specialists. There were no pilots, telemarketers, computer programmers, or even professional athletes. Most of today's jobs are products of the Industrial Age and simply did not exist in the Agrarian Age.

At this moment, you suddenly realize you are not just in a different time and place; you are in a completely new world with a completely different set of rules. And if you are going to survive in this new world, you will need to master its new rules as fast as you can.

You may feel relieved that this is just a thought experiment and that you don't actually have to learn how to live and work in a very different age. However, that sense of relief may be misplaced because, whether you realize it or not, you are in a similar position today with the sudden and rapid emergence of the Digital Age.

In the brief few years since the new millennium began, we have experienced more change than we saw in the last five decades of the previous century. The author Tom Friedman captured this phenomenon succinctly when he recently quipped that, in 2004, "Facebook didn't even exist yet, Twitter was still a sound, the cloud was still in the sky, 4G was a parking space, 'applications' were what you sent to college, LinkedIn was barely known and most people thought it was a prison, Big Data was a good name for a rap star, and Skype, for most people, was a typographical error."[1] None of these things existed just a few years ago, yet each of these innovations is now a staple of our day-to-day lives. We don't need to step into a time machine to transport ourselves to a new world with new rules; we just need to be residents of the early twenty-first century.

Few of us would disagree that we are living in a time of significant change. Change is happening at a pace that most of us find difficult to absorb. A few decades ago, none of us envisioned that driverless cars would be possible in the twenty-first century's second decade. Not even the fiction screenwriters of *Back to the Future*, who presciently anticipated the Chicago Cubs winning the World Series, saw that one coming. When the world is changing more rapidly than we can take it in, it's not surprising that so many of us feel overwhelmed. And, as frazzled as we may sometimes feel, what's most troubling is that our fast-forward world shows no signs of letting up. In fact, with the forthcoming emergence of the Internet of Things, artificial intelligence, robotics, 3D printing, and blockchain technology, the one certainty in an increasingly uncertain world is that the pace of change will only get faster. As hard as it may be to accept, there will probably be more change in the next decade than we have seen in the last twenty-five years.

If we're going to get to a place where we can learn how to absorb change as fast as it happens, we need to understand the full extent of how the digital revolution is transforming the world. And the first thing we need to grasp is that digital transformation is far more than a technology revolution. It is also a sociological revolution that has generated an unprecedented capacity for mass collaboration and created new possibilities for how humans work together. How do we know this? Because this is exactly what happened at the start of the Industrial Revolution when the physical technology of the assembly line and its new capacity for mass production brought about a revolution in how people worked.

ORGANIZING LARGE NUMBERS OF PEOPLE

Before mass production, all business was small business, and the average size of the typical enterprise was four workers.[2] You might be surprised to learn that before the Industrial Revolution, there were no bosses or subordinates; there were only workers. The arrangement of supervisors and subordinates into hierarchical organizations is part of the social architecture that emerged with the Industrial Revolution when, for the first time, businesses needed to come to grips with the challenge of organizing the work of large numbers of people. In its time, mass production brought about a significant leap in work efficiency because it made centralization more efficient, but only if businesses could effectively organize large numbers.

Today, we are witnessing the next great leap in work efficiency as the new digital technologies of mass collaboration make decentralization more efficient. Accordingly, mass collaboration will define the Digital Age like mass production defined the Industrial Age. This means that every company must ask itself, "How will mass collaboration reshape my business?" When it answers that question, it will quickly learn you can't manage mass collaboration businesses using mass production practices, and organizing the work of large numbers of people is an entirely different challenge from what we have been used to.

For well over a hundred years, the assembly line with its hierarchical architecture has served as the prototypical model for managing multitudes of workers. From the very beginning, the Industrial Age was boss-driven and dominated by giants whose names remain familiar today: Carnegie, Rockefeller, and Ford. These "captains of industry" built huge, centralized organizations based on the principles of vertical integration. Control was paramount to the Industrial Age corporation, and vertical integration gave organizations maximum control. Vertical integration also provided the solid foundation for building the command-and-control structures that defined the twentieth-century corporation and reinforced the role of bosses and the tasks they assigned as the focus of work.

The Digital Age is quite different. First, it is customer driven. Keeping the bosses happy is no longer enough. Today, we work for the customers, and these shoppers are increasingly likely to be knowledge workers. This means that somebody else's knowledge workers are your customers. These educated consumers have high expectations, much information, and many choices. They are far more demanding than the bosses would ever dare to be and will readily exercise their options when their expectations are not met. That is why the days of working for the bosses and "just stick to your job" are over. Today, we work for the customers, and keeping them happy is the job. The question is no longer "Who's the boss?" It's now "Who's the customer?"

THE MANAGEMENT GAP

Managing at the new pace of change in the Digital Age requires more agile and flexible organizations that can rapidly adapt to new market demands. This often means that business leaders must be highly competent at forming joint ventures and business partnerships of

4

allied but independently owned organizations that can quickly and seamlessly configure themselves to deliver what's most important to customers. Because managers in these innovative arrangements often do not have command authority over many of the people essential to business success, they find themselves in a most challenging conundrum: How do you manage when you have no practical authority over many geographically dispersed workers in fast-changing markets?

Unfortunately, because they refuse to acknowledge the market shift from bosses to customers, many managers fail to recognize the problem and create a severe management gap for their companies as they continue to act out an obsolete organizational discipline. They remain largely unaware of the new management challenge. That's because they continue to view the world through the social lens of an entrenched mindset that believes operational efficiency is the foundation for building a sustainable competitive advantage and that traditional organization charts still accurately reflect the work we do and the way we work.

For over a century, building a sustainable competitive advantage has been considered the coveted "brass ring" of business success. Blockbuster, Circuit City, Kodak, Sears, Sports Authority, and Radio Shack had all reached the pinnacle—with Circuit City making the cut of the eleven companies featured in Jim Collins's book *Good to Great*—yet each of these twentieth-century giants went bankrupt in our new century. If these great companies can suddenly disappear, it begs the question: In a rapidly changing world, is it possible for a company to create a sustainable competitive advantage?

In the twentieth century, business leaders believed the secret to corporate growth and longevity was finding a way to differentiate your products from your competitors and exploiting that difference to sustain the advantage. This exploitation is accomplished by rigorously safeguarding proprietary knowledge stocks, maximizing cost efficiencies, and constructing barriers to entry to hold off current and potential competitors. This way of thinking was the unquestioned conventional wisdom for achieving market dominance for decades.

Thinking Differently

Chris Anderson, however, disagrees with the conventional wisdom. Anderson, the former editor of *Wired* magazine, is a highly successful entrepreneur who, in addition to his well-known publishing interests, has also dabbled in open-source ventures. One such venture is ArduPilot, an open-source platform able to control autonomous multicopters, fixed-wing aircraft, traditional helicopters, and ground rovers. In his book, *Makers: The New Industrial Revolution*, Anderson relates the story of what happened when, in late 2010, several members of the ArduPilot design community noticed that Chinese clones of their products were for sale in various online marketplaces and how, when asked by the community members what he was going to do about this blatant "piracy," Anderson stunned them when he responded that he was inclined to do nothing.[3]

Anderson's unconventional response reflects his understanding that the digital revolution has radically shifted business's core dynamics and axioms. The most dramatic consequence of this shift is that technological advances over the past two decades have made knowledge an increasingly important—if not the most important—economic asset. This is significant because knowledge is uniquely different from other types of economic assets.

Unlike other natural resources, knowledge is not scarce. Knowledge is an abundant resource and is most valuable when combined with other knowledge. The only way it grows is by giving it away. Thus, holding knowledge as proprietary is counterproductive because it diminishes its value over time. Although it may seem counterintuitive, when knowledge is shared, everyone's intelligence is increased, and all the contributors receive more than they give away.

With this understanding in mind, when Anderson discovered the clones were the work of a single individual who went by the name of "Hazy," he gave the supposed "pirate" edit permission to the community's wiki. He was impressed with the quality of Hazy's Chinese translation of the instruction manual and, given that the operating license of open-source communities means that any work performed by any member is available to all the members, Anderson saw no harm in adding the pirate's voice to the ArduPilot community.

With his new credentials, Hazy proceeded to enhance the product by integrating a seamless Chinese translation of the manual onto the official site. Once that was complete, he surprised Anderson by making quality corrections to the English manual, working through the issues list, and fixing bugs that others were too busy to handle. Hazy quickly became one of ArduPilot's best development team members. By fully including an apparent competitor in the open-source community as a collaborator, the product's Chinese and English versions were substantially enhanced.

Anderson's unusual approach to apparent piracy provides an essential lesson on how the emergence of abundant economic assets is transforming many of the traditional tenets of business. We need to rethink what we mean when we say knowledge is power. In the past, this power was maintained by safeguarding proprietary information and being in a position to have knowledge no one else has. However, a natural consequence of proprietary power is the development of that knowledge is stunted because it remains in the hands of a few people. Meanwhile, one company gains an advantage over others by hoarding and exploiting its knowledge.

Before the digital revolution, hoarding knowledge was a workable business strategy for cornering markets and preserving steady profits because business leaders had the wherewithal to do so. However, that's all changed thanks to the digital revolution, which has dramatically increased the velocity of the exchange of information. Today, knowledge flows are far more valuable than knowledge stocks because, in a post-digital world, the return on assets is far greater on knowledge flows.

This new understanding of knowledge assets is the foundation behind Apple's remarkable success. The iPhone is a platform designed for knowledge flows, which are popularly known as apps. Anyone is free to build an app, and when an app succeeds, both Apple and the developer win. Innovative companies like Apple are making it difficult for traditionally minded companies to build sustainable competitive advantage because the innovators' products have radically reduced the barriers to entry. Today, all an entrepreneur needs to disrupt a market is a good idea, an iPhone, and a credit card as we've seen recently with the rapid rise of Uber. Clearly, the rules for building business and product models in the Digital Age radically differ from the norms that guided constructing models in the Industrial Age.

A Watershed Moment

The digital revolution is a watershed moment in human history because its technological innovations are not only changing how we build business models, but perhaps more importantly, it has made it possible for a radically different organizational model—the distributed peer-to-peer network—to be what it never could before: a practical form of social organization. Digital technology has provided the ubiquitous means for people to self-organize within the context of hyper-connected networks in ways none of us could have imagined a mere two decades ago. For example, who would have thought that the world's largest reference work would be a self-organized effort of volunteers working without assignments and pay? At the start of our new millennium, none of us could have conceived of an enterprise like Wikipedia. After all, how would anything get done if no one was in charge? Surely, such an enterprise would be powerless and doomed.

As we know, things did not turn out as we might have expected at the time. The Wikipedia self-organized network didn't just survive; it thrived and created a level of productivity far beyond anyone's expectations. Additionally, without any intention to do so, it ended the reign of the 244-year-old market leader within a mere decade. How did this bossless networked enterprise become so powerful? It did so by applying the new rules of our new world. In the world as we have previously known it, Wikipedia could never happen.

One of the most consequential developments of the Digital Age is that centralized, hierarchical organizations that leverage the individual intelligence of an elite few are being displaced by a new breed of business leaders designing their organizations as highly

8

sophisticated distributed networks capable of rapidly leveraging human and artificial collective intelligence. This architectural shift is far more transformative than most managers realize because the vast majority lack an understanding of the dynamics of networks. Unfortunately, our knowledge deficiencies in the ways of networks cause us to significantly underestimate the magnitude of the transformation and its related exponential rate of change.

This growing knowledge gap is problematic because hierarchies and networks are neither equal nor interchangeable structures. Networks tend to outperform hierarchies by a wide margin in terms of both intelligence and speed because, by leveraging the collective intelligence of the many rather than the individual smarts of the elite few, networks dramatically accelerate the path to knowledge. The natural propensity of networks to leverage collective intelligence is the great game changer and, arguably, the most critical consequence of digital transformation because it is a new and far more powerful form of intelligence.

One of the consequences of this game changer is that it transforms the foundation for building a sustainable competitive advantage. In the Digital Age, this capacity shifts from those companies that maintain the status quo through extraordinary cost and operational efficiencies to those who create the future by rapidly adapting their business and product models to keep pace with accelerating change. Put simply, in the Industrial Age, if you couldn't maintain, you couldn't survive; in the Digital Age, you won't survive if you can't adapt.

The inability to make this shift may explain why so many businesses are suddenly disappearing. In the 1950s, the average age of a company on the S&P 500 Index was sixty years.[4] Today, that number has been reduced to less than twenty years, and by 2027, the average tenure is expected to shrink to just twelve years.[5] To put this in perspective, more than half the companies in the Fortune 500 at the start of the twenty-first century no longer exist.[6] This includes well-known names like Sears, Mattress Factory, Brookstone,

Rockport, Nine West, Bon Ton, Toys "R" Us, Payless, The Limited, Sports Authority, and Radio Shack.[7]

The sudden emergence of a highly networked digital world represents the most significant inflection point in the history of business. In a mere two decades, this phenomenon has been far more transformative far more quickly than anything we've experienced in the now-gone Industrial Age.

For example, in the mid-1990s, the five most valuable companies were General Electric, Royal Dutch Shell, the Coca-Cola Company, NTT (Nippon Telegraph and Telephone), and ExxonMobil.[8] These were all traditional Industrial Age enterprises that leveraged operational and cost efficiencies to sustain their market positions. Two decades later, the top-five list was completely revamped and included Apple, Google, Microsoft, Amazon, and Facebook.[9] Each of these companies is a Digital Age innovator that is rewriting the rules for how successful companies thrive by relying upon distributed networks rather than centralized hierarchies to master the challenges of keeping pace with a rapidly changing world.

Social Architecture

If business leaders want to sustain their organizations in this radically different business landscape, they will need to fully appreciate the dual dimensions of what has come to be known as digital transformation. While most business leaders understand that innovations in digital technology are transforming business models and supply chains, they fail to understand that this disruptive revolution is also profoundly remodeling the social architecture for how we work together in large organizations.

When we think of architecture, what comes to mind are beautiful buildings or elaborate edifices. We rarely think of architecture as something that explains how societies, economies, or organizations work. And yet, without social architecture, much of what we experience in everyday life would not be possible.

A fundamental social architecture must answer two questions: 1) How does power work? and 2) How do things get done? In hierarchies, power belongs to those in charge, and things get done through the application of centralized control mechanisms. Thus, in organizing the work of large numbers of people, hierarchical structures leverage the individual intelligence of the bosses at the top of an organization. However, in networks, power belongs to the connected, and things get done through the application of collective intelligence dynamics, which enable self-organization of work among large numbers of people.

The shift from hierarchies to networks will not be easy for traditional leaders because the ways that power and intelligence work are radically transformed. For leaders who have climbed the corporate ladder by demonstrating their superior intelligence and are very comfortable with leading by being in charge, cultivating the organization's collective intelligence and trusting the synergistic power of self-organization will feel completely counterintuitive.

Nevertheless, peer-to-peer networks are the future of organizational work. This is because, in the coming decade, the pace of digital transformation will exponentially accelerate as we experience two of the most far-reaching events in human history: the connection of all humans and things via the Internet of Things (IoT) and the proliferation of human collective intelligence via sophisticated artificial intelligence (AI) systems. These events will result in an exponential leap in human intelligence as we gain access to the extraordinary speed and capacity of collective intelligence. And, whether we like it or not, they will inevitably and radically change our understanding of how organizations work.

Digital transformation is a disruptive evolution that requires organizational leaders to adopt entirely new ways of thinking and acting if they want to lead sustainable enterprises. Those incapable or unwilling to learn new ways risk finding themselves out of a job or, worse yet, their companies out of business. This may explain why so many legacy businesses are failing or becoming extinct. However, those who have the courage and the wherewithal to think differently have the opportunity to build organizations that excel at changing as fast as the world around them.

New Ways of Thinking

Thinking differently begins by letting go of an old mental model and embracing a new paradigm for understanding how organizations work. For over three centuries, the machine was the dominant metaphor that shaped the mindset of Industrial Age thinking. This mechanistic mental model was a useful guide for navigating the challenges of a relatively predictable world where the pace of technological change was slower than our human capacity to adapt to change. When the world is seen as a machine, it is natural that the architecture of our social organizations takes the form of top-down hierarchies. This explains why the typical organizational chart looks like a mechanical schematic. And as long as the pace of change is slower than our ability to adapt to change, mechanistic mindsets are practical tools for interpreting how the world works. Despite its obvious annoyances, the bureaucratic organization is an important—if not the most important—innovation of the Industrial Age because it solved the unprecedented challenge of coordinating the work of vast numbers of people. And, arguably, because it was also the economic engine that created the middle class.

However, one consequence of the sudden emergence of accelerating change is that industrial age bureaucracies are no longer practical tools for organizing large numbers. According to Eric Teller, the CEO of Google's X research and development lab, somewhere in the past decade, we crossed the point where the pace of technological change now exceeds our human capacity to adapt to change.[10] That's why the transformation into a hyper-connected world is the most significant inflection point in human history and why the machine is no longer a workable metaphor for how the world works.

Once all the computers were connected and the network became firmly rooted, the world and its problems suddenly became more challenging and beyond the solution capacities of linear, mechanistic models. But more importantly, a new dominant metaphor emerged that's a better fit for a connected world: the network. The morphing of social metaphors explains why this inflection point is more a sociological than a technological revolution. Digital transformation is a paradigm shift in how we view and solve problems when the world changes faster than we can absorb in real time.

While most business leaders today have not rushed to embrace new ways of working together—preferring instead to hold onto their hierarchical power and control—their customers have been fascinated by the newfound power that mass collaboration networks provided them. Companies that produced digitized products, such as music and videos, were particularly vulnerable to self-organized networked activity as their customers began exchanging digital files via Napster's online web application. Although the music industry was able to shut Napster down, it was ultimately helpless against the forces of change: CDs and music stores quickly gave way to digital downloads and iTunes. The media and entertainment industries' longstanding business and operating models have been permanently and radically transformed. Stalwart names, such as Border's, Blockbuster, Kodak, Tower Records, and the Encyclopedia Britannica, have been disrupted or displaced by the upstarts of Amazon, Netflix, Apple, Spotify, and Wikipedia. Keeping up with customers who have discovered how to use networks to change as fast as the world around them is one more reason legacy organizational leaders must embrace new ways of working together.

Transformation Is Not an Option

As the world becomes increasingly networked, solving the problems of a hyper-connected world will require a higher level of thinking. One of Albert Einstein's most famous quotes is, "We can't solve problems by using the same level of thinking we used when we created them." This is especially true today because the phenomenon of digital transformation is rapidly shifting the basic context of our problems and challenges from the complicated to the complex.

Complicated problems, such as designing and building an automobile, can be solved by employing mechanical thinking and hierarchical division of labor because machines don't evolve, and fixed blueprints work as reliable guides. However, solving complex problems, such as staying one step ahead of disruptive technologies, discovering new ways to create economic value for those whose jobs are eliminated by automation, or restoring security to obsolescent systems that fall prey to an increasing army of hackers, will require a higher level of thinking than our mechanistic models provide. It requires a deep understanding of networks and how they work.

When the pace of change is continually accelerating, it becomes painfully clear that no single individual, or even a small group of experts, is smart enough to process all that is happening in real time. If you want to manage successfully in the world of mass collaboration, you inevitably learn that nobody is smarter than everybody and that collective wisdom is more valuable than conventional wisdom. After all, it was the conventional wisdom of an elite few that created the financial meltdown that became the Great Recession. If we had had the foresight and the capacity to tap into the collective knowledge of all the managers and workers in the financial services industry, it is doubtful that their collective wisdom would have reinforced the conventional wisdom that extending zero-down, low-document mortgages to high-risk borrowers would make for a winning strategy.

The most untapped resource in corporate America today is the collective intelligence of an organization's workers. What is amazing is that accessing this abundant reservoir requires no investment in dollars because it's already paid for. What it does require is the development of innovative collective learning processes that employ a radically different social architecture when we bring people together inside organizations. Given the ever-widening gap between the advances in twenty-first-century systems technology and the stagnation of a century-old social architecture, it's just a matter of time before all of us will be asking the question that is causing so many twentysomethings to turn their backs on traditional companies today: "Why, when we can quickly collaborate in cyberspace with all kinds of people from all over the globe, is it so hard to get anything done whenever we get together in the same room?" The answer to this question requires us to take a deeper look at how we view and hold power.

TRANSFORMING POWER

Whether an organization is effective or not is all about power. Effective organizations are influential players who are able to shape the world when they can and have the wherewithal to quickly adapt when they can't. Ineffective organizations are those that are powerless in the face of complex or challenging circumstances. If you want to be the leader of an effective organization, you need to be highly skillful in the use of power.

Unfortunately, power generally has a bad reputation, and most of us tend to think of power in a negative light. That's because our typical experiences with power are inside hierarchical organizations where power is equated with control. However, in actuality, power is neutral; it is neither good nor bad. Whether we experience power as positive or negative often reflects the quality of our relationships. That's because power is always interpersonal and only exists within the context of relationships. In hierarchical organizations, power is generally ascribed by position, with those few in higher positions having more authority than the many in the lower ranks. Thus, most of us perceive the exercise of authority as about being in charge and having power *over* people.

However, the technology revolution is radically reshaping how power is exercised, especially in large organizations. The late psychologist Abraham Maslow observed that the most effective leaders invest in power *with* rather than power *over* people.[11] Our early experiences with online collaborations demonstrate that Maslow's observation also holds true for organizations. Open-source platforms, such as Linux, Craigslist, and eBay, are not interested in exerting control or having power over people. These twenty-first-century businesses understand that, in today's fast-paced world, the best companies are those that build platforms to share power with people. By building networked structures to aggregate and leverage the collective intelligence of the many, these mass collaboration enterprises can redefine whole industries and easily outperform their traditional counterparts.

Leaders of these innovative enterprises understand that power with people is much more effective than power over people, especially when organizations must manage at the speed of change to remain competitive. They also understand that, in a post-digital world, the basis of power for effective leadership rapidly shifts from "being in charge" to "being connected." Executive power no longer comes from dominating the thinking or directing the work of others; it now comes from integrating the best of everyone's ideas and leveraging mass collaboration platforms. In contrast to traditional hierarchies, which limit the interpersonal influence of the many through the ascription of authority, the power structures of digital-age companies amplify the opportunities for developing relationships across all people within an organizational network. The more connections there are, the quicker a business can access and leverage its collective intelligence.

In our hyper-connected world, power does not come from amassing control but from co-creating shared understanding. When co-creation rather than control is the fundamental way things get done, being in charge is meaningless because an effective, shared understanding can never be mandated. Shared understanding is something that must be facilitated and created by consensus.

The most significant leadership challenge for today's corps of business leaders is shifting how they approach power. If they continue to insist that power is a function of being in charge, they are likely to fall victim to the consequences of a world that is changing much faster than their organizations. If they can accept that power in an increasingly networked world is a function of being connected, they and their organizations will become highly skilled in adapting to a rapidly changing world successfully.

A New Organizational Challenge

Today's new decentralized organizations will create pressure for hierarchical companies to become more flexible and nimble if they hope to compete in the new economy. As it becomes more common for managers to be accountable for initiatives where they have no direct reporting relationship with many of the key staff on the project team, managing by control is not an option. When critical staff work for another company in the business alliance or another country on the other side of the globe, collaboration based on shared understanding becomes necessary for getting the job done. This requires a substantial shift in management skills and competencies.

Letting go of the exercise of control, which is at the heart of traditional hierarchical management, and learning how to lead by cultivating a highly effective shared understanding among collaborative teams will require substantial growth on the part of managers. They must adopt entirely new ways of thinking, behaving, and managing.

To demonstrate this point, let us once again return to our thought experiment. This time, imagine you are with a group of top executives who travel to Dublin, Ireland, ten years into the future. As you land on the rolling hills of the Emerald Isle, the captain once again informs you that you are now permanent residents of this future world because of a malfunction in your vehicle. However, she also notifies you that she has radioed ahead, and a group of job recruiters will be meeting the time machine to help secure work for you and your colleagues in this new time and place. As you consider your predicament, you feel fairly confident that, despite the ten-year difference, you should be able to find work as an executive. After all, management is management, and you are an expert at running large organizations.

As you descend from the time machine, you and your colleagues are divided into smaller groups, and your group is greeted by a recruiter who takes you to one corner of a huge room for your interviews. As you wait your turn, you can overhear the recruiter's conversation with one of your fellow executives. In response to the recruiter's inquiry about his executive qualifications, your colleague proudly relates stories of his ability to take charge, effectively exert authority over people, and get workers to do what needs to be done. After he finishes, the recruiter appears puzzled as she comments, "But I thought you said you were a skilled business leader? The skills you describe are suitable for placement as a manager of a small store or perhaps a prison guard—but not a leader in a large organization." As the recruiter sees the confusion on your colleague's face, she explains, "A lot has changed in the last ten years. In today's large organizations, we are looking for leaders who are highly skilled facilitators and great consensus builders. Do you have any experience as a facilitative leader or examples of where you were able to use consensus management as a competitive advantage?"

As your colleague sits silently, you can see he suddenly realizes that he may only be ten years into the future but is in a completely different world. He is now clearly living in the Digital Age, and it is evident that the rules of the game have changed. Only then can he see beyond his mental boundaries as he suddenly discovers that he is most certainly ill equipped when it comes to managing in the new networked world.

As we enter these first days of a new age, we are indeed at a tipping point in the evolution of management, where traditional executives find themselves in an unprecedented business reality for which they are totally unprepared. This means that the single greatest threat to the survival of many businesses over the next decade may very well be their managers. For proof, we need to look no further than the long list of stalwart companies over the last two decades that have vanished because of the myopic decision-making of an elite few.

The new economy of the Digital Age is all about change—continuous, unrelenting change. If business leaders want to successfully manage in a fast-moving world, they must embrace a very different mindset and design their organizations as highly intelligent, self-managed peer-to-peer networks.

Unfortunately, given the accelerating pace of change in this new economy, there isn't much time to transition. However, for those leaders who are ready to take the leap, there are companies whose different ways of thinking and acting are better aligned with the twenty-first century's new network mindset. It turns out that designing self-managed peer-to-peer networks is not new. In fact, several of the model companies in this book had the foresight to recognize the power of collaboration well before the Internet and have been practicing this alternative management approach for more than sixty years. What is new is that rather than being the exception, self-managed networks will likely become the organizational norm by the end of the next decade.

This will not necessarily be an easy transformation for traditional business leaders because the norms and values of hierarchical management are deeply ingrained. Hierarchical management is a mindset passed on from generation to generation of managers through the informal socialization habits of corporate cultures. Accordingly, as with most mindsets, managers are largely unaware of why they do what they do. They just know that's how it's always been done and assume that's the way it is.

Because behavioral change is as much about letting go of old ways as it is about learning new habits, we must first become aware of why managers do what they do. In the next chapter, we will take a short detour from the book's central theme and provide a quick synopsis of the origins and thinking behind the principles, processes, and practices of command-and-control management. Hopefully, by raising our awareness of the roots of a century-old management architecture, we will better understand why it worked for so long and, more importantly, why it will no longer work in a digitally transformed world.

2

AN IDEA WHOSE TIME HAS PASSED

So often, in making behavior changes, it's not learning new practices that presents the greatest challenge but letting go of old habits that proves to be the most difficult. This is because old behaviors are so second nature that we don't have to think about them; we do them automatically, often unconsciously. Letting go of traditional management practices will be very difficult because the assumptions and beliefs of hierarchical management have become so deeply ingrained over the one-hundred-fifty-year life of the modern corporation.

If you were to peruse the catalogs of most university business schools, you are not likely to find a course entitled "Command-and-Control Management." A deeply ingrained paradigm doesn't need to be taught. In fact, the curriculum of most business schools is focused either on strategic analysis or technical expertise, such as marketing, finance, or information systems. This may explain why so many MBA graduates, especially those from top-tier schools, work as management consultants rather than corporate executives.

There are also no training programs inside corporations that specifically teach an overview of the hierarchical management discipline. There may be courses that focus on an aspect of command and control, such as performance management, but there are no comprehensive corporate programs on the overall traditional model. Even the American Management Association (AMA), which provides extensive national training programs, does not offer a specific course on command-and-control management. Quite the contrary, the curricula of the leading management and leadership training organizations such as the AMA, the Center for Creative Leadership, and FranklinCovey are focused on how not to be command-and-control managers!

Nevertheless, despite the millions of dollars spent on these training programs and the absence of formal training in the traditional model, hierarchical management practices remain deeply embedded in most organizations' corporate "DNA." Even considering its historical success throughout the twentieth century, the staying power of command-and-control management is nothing short of incredible when you consider all the literature and evidence supporting alternative approaches and all the money organizations invest in training on the latest trends in humanistic management practices. It begs the question: If nobody likes command-and-control management, why is it so commonly practiced?

THREE EARLY BUSINESS THINKERS

To answer this question, let's go back to the early 1900s when the Industrial Age enveloped the Western world. While the origins of the command-and-control model can be traced back to military practice, the development, evolution, and adaptation of this model to the newly emerging concept of the corporation were heavily influenced by three business thinkers whose work and ideas were the drivers for the productivity expansion that accelerated the Industrial Age.

Frederick W. Taylor developed the philosophy that guided the evolution of the modern corporation throughout the twentieth century. Taylor advocated a systematic quantitative approach known as scientific management, designed to improve workers' efficiency and productivity significantly. An engineer by training, Taylor believed that there was one right way to do each job and that it was management's responsibility, by applying scientific methods such as time and motion studies, to discover the best way to perform each task and develop the appropriate standard methods for workers to follow. He aimed to design an organizational structure that would make people as reliable and efficient as machines.

The fundamental structural element of Taylor's organizational model is the class distinction between managers and staff that continues to this day. He drew a sharp divide between managers and workers, with managers responsible for applying scientific principles in the planning and engineering of work. In contrast, workers needed only to concern themselves with performing their assigned tasks. Taylor held workers in low regard, believing that they were incapable of understanding how best to carry out even the simplest of tasks. He firmly believed that workers required close supervision if work was to be done right. The rapid and broad acceptance of scientific management practices led to the establishment of the many rules and canons that eventually evolved into the modern policies and procedures manuals that continue to give precedence to management protocol over individual judgment.

Taylor's philosophy took root in the newly emerging American corporations because it immediately resulted in tremendous productivity gains, and everyone was making money. Increased production drove greater profits for the corporate owners, and equally important, even though scientific management treated workers as nothing more than machines who needed to be made efficient, these workers realized higher and more stable wages than when they worked as independent craftsmen or on farms.

The relatively higher wages necessary to induce worker compliance with imposed work standards laid the foundation for the expansion of the middle class throughout the twentieth century. While many have deplored Taylor and his methods—indeed, "Taylorism" has become a pejorative term—scientific management resulted in a productivity explosion that expansively improved the standard of living for whole societies. The business author Aaron Dignan notes, "Since the publication of Taylor's *Principles* in 1911, the percent of people living in extreme poverty has gone from 82.4 percent to just 9.6 percent."[1] The influence of Taylor's approach was so pervasive that the management guru Peter Drucker described scientific management as "the one American philosophy that has swept the world—more so even than the Constitution and the Federalist papers."[2]

Taylor changed how the world thought about organizing all forms of social organization. He spawned a mental revolution that shaped how we think about organizing the world and, equally importantly, how we think about solving problems.[3] More than a hundred years later, we continue to believe that planning and control are the core tasks of management.

While Taylor provided the ideological framework, Henry Ford supplied the practical engine that drove the modern corporation. Before the twentieth century, goods were produced by individual craftsmen on an item-by-item basis. Ford completely revolutionized manufacturing with his development of the assembly line, which quickly became the most advanced application of Taylor's philosophy at the time. The production of automobiles was engineered into a sequence of discrete activities, with each worker assigned a specific task at a specific location as products moved along a conveyor belt. The assembly line dramatically increased worker output by forcing workers to toil at a set pace on a single task. It wasn't long before Henry Ford's mass production concept, which was quickly adopted by other automobile makers, became the standard for all manufacturing industries. The resulting growth in the production capacity of American factories is often credited with creating and fueling the modern consumer culture.

With Taylor's philosophy firmly taking hold in the factories of the early twentieth century, the stage was set for the formulation of the new discipline of corporate management. Until this time, apart from the military, work was generally organized around smaller numbers of people. The farm was a family enterprise, and those who engaged in crafts or professions worked either as individual practitioners or in small local firms.

With the expansion of the railroads in the late nineteenth century and the development of large factories in the early twentieth century, there was a need for businesses to organize large numbers of workers for the first time in history. Until this time, administering the business and doing the work were generally performed by the same people. However, when a new socioeconomic age is born, it changes the work we do and the way we work. This was evident as the Industrial Age took root. The advent of scientific management and the invention of the assembly line created the need to separate the administration from the technical performance of the business.

While Taylor is the first to draw the distinction between management and staff, Frenchman Henri Fayol first recognized management as a distinct discipline. Fayol lays the theoretical foundation for the application of command-and-control as the framework for this new discipline by codifying the five fundamental responsibilities of centralized management: planning, organizing, directing, coordinating, and controlling. Fayol also articulates the guiding principles for effectively managing the top-down hierarchical organization, many of which we will recognize from our organizational experiences. These include the principle of division of labor, where Fayol reinforces Taylor's thinking that efficient production is only possible if work is divided into specialized tasks. The principle of authority and responsibility specifies that authority is the manager's right to command others to do a job and that with this authority comes the manager's responsibility to get the job done. The principles of unity of command and unity of direction postulate that each person has only one supervisor and that there should only be one manager for a particular set of objectives. Lastly, the scalar principle calls for a ranking of authority and clear communication protocols among the various organizational members. This principle means that certain decisions can only be made by certain levels, and when communicating vertically within an organization, the chain of command must always be respected.

If you were to shadow the typical executive in a traditional organization today, you would find that just about everything the manager does fits into one of Fayol's five fundamental responsibilities. Work plans and timelines, job descriptions and organization charts, directives and assignments, meetings and conference calls, status reports, and performance appraisals—these activities make up a typical manager's day. In defining these activities as the essential work of management, Fayol reinforced Taylor's premise that the primary goal of an organizational model is to make the large group efforts of humans as efficient as machines.

The Downsides of Scientific Management

The breakthrough innovation behind Taylor's organizational model was in applying the scientific thinking of the time to the task of coordinating large group efforts. In the late nineteenth century, Isaac Newton's reductionist principles shaped our understanding of how the world worked. Newton saw the world as a machine that followed absolute physical laws. Newton's principles fostered a worldview that believed we could manipulate our world if we understood and applied these laws to navigate our day-to-day lives. This worldview was the catalyst for the myriad inventions that ushered in the Industrial Revolution. In applying this worldview to business, Taylor advanced the idea that scientific principles could be the foundation for assuring predictable future results for large organizations. Accordingly, as the top-down hierarchy was rapidly adopted as the default management model, central planning was established as the foundation for strategy, and control became the focus of execution.

From a financial perspective, this model worked exceedingly well throughout the twentieth century when the pace of change was much slower than today. And while workers continue to share in this prosperity as the wages paid by corporations allow large numbers of families to enjoy middle-class lives, there are downsides to making people as efficient as machines.

One problem is the dehumanization of the work experience, which often results in low employee engagement. According to a recent Gallup survey, only 34 percent of employees are engaged in their work, which means two out of every three workers are going through the motions and are not active contributors in the workplace.[4] When workers are treated like cogs in a machine, and the expectation is that they should do what they're told and not question authority, we should not be surprised at the low level of worker engagement.

Another downside of top-down hierarchies is that they are heavily biased to maintain the status quo. In a relatively stable world, this can be a manageable problem because there's ample time to shift strategy if the pace of market change moves slowly. However, in rapidly changing times, the status quo bias can be fatal because bureaucracies tend to kill the innovation capacity that is needed to adapt to fast-moving markets. This was the fate of a well-known market leader that was once a household name.

A Failure to Adapt

In late 1999, Michael Schrage, a business innovation consultant, was hired by the video rental giant Blockbuster to help the company address a nagging customer service issue. Market surveys convincingly showed Blockbuster's executives that they had many angry customers who hated late fees, or what the company preferred to call "extended viewing" fees.[5] Unfortunately, the data indicated that most of these unhappy renters were their best customers. Schrage's challenge was to suggest ways to transform these prolific video watchers into happy customers while maintaining the company's lucrative profit margins.

Schrage's task would not be easy because late fees were a major source of the company's revenue. In fact, Blockbuster often designed promotions to optimize late fees by offering customers two or three videos for the price of one, anticipating that many of these "free" rentals would be returned late.[6] Although these revenues were easy money, they were risky profits because they were made at the customer's expense and, thus, could quickly disappear if angry customers found a better alternative.

In exploring ways to retain Blockbuster's best customers, Schrage designed an experiment in which a representative sample of a dozen stores would ask customers if they would like to provide their email addresses and receive reminders a day before the due date. At the time, companies did not routinely gather email addresses as they do today. The return rates and late fees for the experimental group would be compared against a control sample of comparable stores to measure the effect of this potential policy change on revenue.[7]

Anticipating that mitigating customer anger was likely to reduce late fee revenue, Schrage thought the collection of customer email addresses could also open future possibilities for increased customer engagement, leading to happier customers and increased rental revenue to offset diminished late fees.

When Schrage presented his proposal to the Blockbuster executives, he was stunned by their response. They were not interested in finding new ways to make customers happy. They wanted to preserve their product model and its lucrative late fees. They had expected Schrage to devise a solution that would help customers see extended viewing fees as a good value for the option of viewing flexibility. As Schrage attempted to convince the executives of the value of his proposed experiment, they became hostile. According to Schrage, they protested, "Why on earth do we want to remind customers the day before to return their movies on time? Why should we test an idea that's virtually guaranteed to reduce our profitability? How will this help us make up for the money we'd lose?"[8]

Like every other company that feels it has built a product model that gives it a sustainable competitive advantage, the Blockbuster executives were heavily invested in maintaining the status quo. After all, in 1999, Blockbuster was the dominant market leader in the United States. Its competitors were mostly local video operators with limited movie selections. The video giant easily dominated the competition because, with over 6,500 locations, there was a Blockbuster store with a wide selection of videos within a ten-minute drive of virtually every neighborhood within the United States.[9] Given their strong market position, the Blockbuster executives were convinced it was customer attitude and not the company product model that needed to be changed. The executives were so displeased with Schrage's proposal that the consultant felt compelled to apologize for wasting the executives' time and waived his fee.[10]

A few months later, in early 2000, Reed Hastings and Marc Randolph would bring a different proposal to John Antioco, Blockbuster's CEO. Three years earlier, Hastings and Randolph founded an internet-based startup called Netflix that delivered DVDs by mail using a monthly subscription model. For a flat fee, members received unlimited movies without per-title rental fees, due dates, or late fees. Although the Netflix founders were convinced the internet was the future of home entertainment, the startup was off to a rocky start with only three hundred thousand subscribers and on its way to $57 million in losses for the year.[11] Hastings and Randolph offered to sell Netflix to Blockbuster for $50 million and develop Blockbuster. com as their online video division. They suggested the combination of the two companies could leverage the value of the Blockbuster brand into an innovative product line that would expand the video giant's market presence and transition the market leader into the next generation of their industry. Antioco was not convinced by the Netflix founders' proposal, declining it on the spot. The Blockbuster CEO saw no value in building an online presence, chiding, "The dot-com hysteria is completely overblown."[12]

When Antioco turned down Netflix's offer, he was at the helm of a well-established $6 billion enterprise that had raised $465 million in a successful IPO the previous year.[13] Its business model seemed secure as Blockbuster continued to grow throughout the decade, debuting on the *Fortune 500* in 2006. The company would remain a fixture on the coveted list for the following four years but would fall off in 2011 after filing for bankruptcy in September 2010 with $1 billion in debt.

It turned out that Antioco couldn't have been more wrong. The internet did become the next generation of home entertainment. Because Antioco couldn't envision a future that could be very different from the past, Blockbuster failed to adapt to a rapidly changing market. Antioco's passing up the opportunity to purchase Netflix would turn out to be Blockbuster's single worst management decision.

On the other hand, Netflix would greatly surpass Blockbuster's short-lived success. After a few years of struggle in the early 2000s,

Netflix's online business model finally connected with the market as more and more people signed up for their DVD subscription model. Over the next two decades, Netflix demonstrated a robust capacity for keeping up with technological change as it morphed from physical DVDs to online streaming and, eventually, movie production. In 2021, the company that offered to sell itself to Blockbuster for $50 million had a market value of over $300 billion.[14]

The Fatal Flaws of Hierarchical Management

Blockbuster's executives didn't fail to adapt because they were bad managers; they failed because they were following what they understood to be good management practices. At the start of our new century, Blockbuster was a fifteen-year-old company that had cornered its market. The video giant's financially successful product model and highly efficient delivery system set the company apart as the clear market leader. Suppose you were a Blockbuster executive working on a three-year strategic plan in 2000. In that case, chances are you, too, would have been biased toward charting a course that maintained what you would have likely seen as a sustainable competitive advantage. After all, if the business plan has been working well for fifteen years and you see nothing in the near future indicating the need for change, it makes sense to stick with the plan. And for the next three years, you would have been right. By the end of 2003, Blockbuster had grown to almost 9,000 locations with healthy earnings on approximately $6 billion in revenue. Few would have argued that Blockbuster wasn't a well-managed company. That's because the management practices the executives were following were doing what they were designed to do: maintain the status quo.

Taylor's management philosophy assumes that the business world and business organizations behave like simple static systems. This reductionistic approach assumes that, like machines, the design objective of management systems is to maintain equilibrium. Thus, managers are imbued with a bias for the status quo and a belief that the primary tasks of management are planning and control.

In a stable world, these primary tasks make sense because business models can be profitable for many decades. However, in a dynamic world, the life cycle of a business model can be reduced to a few years, which means organizations must be very competent at adapting to change. This has become problematic for traditional managers because planning is inherently change resistant, as we saw when Blockbuster's executives reacted hostilely to Schrage's proposed experiment to discover ways to encourage happier customers. Although Schrage was providing Blockbuster with an early warning indicator of how late fees could become potential trouble down the road, this observation was summarily dismissed because it could result in a major shift in what had been a very profitable business model. The executives liked the status quo, felt secure in their competitive position, and had no desire to change.

Traditional management's preoccupation with control reinforces this resistance to change. The business author Gary Hamel notes that, in most languages, the terms "manage" and "control" are synonymous.[15] Hamel accurately points out, "Whatever the rhetoric to the contrary, control is the principle preoccupation of most managers and management systems."[16] When the fundamental organizing principle of a management system is hierarchical control, organizations experience three limiting factors that are relatively benign in static situations but can be fatal in dynamic environments.

The first is the inability to manage complexity. The reductionist tools and practices employed by traditional managers are ill-equipped to handle the challenges of complex problems. The Blockbuster executives were looking for a simplistic solution that would convince its angry customers to appreciate the viewing flexibility they received for the price of the late fees. Schrage's experiment would have focused on the holistic customer experience to find ways to avoid late fees and discover new ways to deliver value that might generate new revenue categories.

Another limiting factor is that hierarchies inherently kill innovation. Given management's status quo bias, people who suggest new ways of doing things—especially if they threaten existing business or product models—typically encounter a bureaucratic gauntlet that few ideas ever survive. Despite the Netflix founders' market insights and their accurate sense of the future of home entertainment, Antioco quickly rejected a brilliant innovation opportunity because he was incapable of imagining how Blockbuster might manage its own evolution.

The final limiting factor is perhaps the most dangerous attribute of command-and-control management: Decision-making is often the prerogative of one person. In top-down hierarchies, single individuals have the authority to make unilateral decisions whose consequences can be far reaching across the business. The single worst decision in Blockbuster's twenty-five-year run was made by one person at the end of one meeting. Had Antioco accepted the offer to acquire Netflix, Blockbuster would likely be a $300 billion company today and still the most popular brand in home entertainment.

Blockbuster's path to eventual bankruptcy began with this one consequential decision. In giving one person the singular authority to make this decision, Blockbuster failed to act intelligently. And this failure would be fatal. Despite conventional thinking, planning and control are not the primary tasks of management because these two activities do not guarantee sustained success. The primary tasks of management are discovery and shared understanding, especially in rapidly changing times.

When the management system is designed around planning and control, it assumes, as Taylor did, that problem-solving is best done by the elite few who can quickly deduce the right answers and put in place an action plan for the staff to follow. When the system is built for discovery and shared understanding, it operates very differently by leveraging the collective intelligence of teams to discover the right questions and, in answering these questions, to deepen their understanding of the best ways to resolve complex problems. While it may seem counterintuitive to shift management's focus away from planning and control to the unfamiliar tasks of discovering and understanding, the managers in one industry learned they had to make this shift because they were literally losing too many lives.

Improving Human Decision Making

On December 28, 1978, United Flight 173 took off from JFK airport in New York bound for Portland, Oregon, with a stopover in Denver. Captain Malburn McBroom, First Officer Rod Beebe, and Engineer Forrest Mendenhall were in the cockpit. The plane landed in Denver on time and without complication. After deplaning the first leg of the flight and boarding the new passengers for the final leg, the DC-8 aircraft pulled away from the gate with enough fuel to cover the flight plus an extra sixty-five minutes in case of an unforeseen delay getting into Portland.

United 173 took off from Denver's Stapleton Airport at 2:47 p.m. with Beebe at the controls and McBroom acting as co-pilot. At 5:00 p.m., the flight neared Portland under ideal landing conditions. As the plane descended to 7,000 feet, Beebe asked for the landing gear down. When McBroom lowered the wheels, a tiny problem popped up: The indicator lamp for the right main landing gear didn't light up. The crew wasn't sure whether the landing gear was locked in place.

At 5:09 p.m., McBroom radioed the tower to report the problem and entered a holding pattern at 5,000 feet to diagnose and handle the situation. This was a relatively minor issue in the scheme of things because if they had to land with the right landing gear collapsing, they might damage a wing, but all the passengers would arrive safely.

McBroom glanced at the gauges, and seeing that there were 12,000 pounds of fuel, he shifted his attention to the landing gear. The crew consulted the thick manual for instructions. They considered retracting and re-extending the gear but feared they could compound the problem. They considered a low pass by the control tower for a visual inspection by the controller but ruled that out because it was dark. At 5:30 p.m., McBroom called United Maintenance in San Francisco. They didn't have any useful information and indicated that the crew had done everything they could. It was now 5:49 p.m., and the crew still didn't know if the right landing gear was locked or not.

McBroom now shifted his attention to contingency plans for a rough landing. As they began to review their checklist, Mendenhall, with concern in his voice, reported that their fuel pump lights were starting to blink. McBroom reassured him that it was alright because the plane was turning, and the pump lights tended to blink with the sloshing of the fuel around the sensors when fuel was low. At 6:06 p.m., McBroom started to tell the tower he expected to land in five minutes, but he didn't finish his sentence because the engine noise had changed. Over the next two minutes, one by one, each of the four engines shut down. The plane had run out of fuel.

McBroom took control of the noiseless jet as it steadily lost altitude. Although it was just eight miles from the runway, the distance was impossible. At 6:13 p.m., Beebe declared a mayday, and at 6:15 p.m., United 173 ripped through two vacant houses and a patch of trees before coming to rest. Because they were out of fuel, there was no fire. Fortunately, 179 of the 189 people on board survived the crash. Among the ten who perished was the flight engineer Mendenhall. McBroom and Beebe both survived.

The crash baffled the aviation community. How could an experienced three-person crew run out of fuel before landing? They had over an hour of spare fuel, a relatively minor technical issue, and clear protocols for dealing with a landing gear failure.

A few months after the crash, the National Transportation Safety Board (NTSB) issued its report. It concluded the plane could have landed safely 30 or 40 minutes after the landing gear malfunction. The cause of the accident was the captain's failure to monitor the plane's fuel state and properly respond to crewmember advisories regarding the fuel state.

This wasn't a simple case of pilot error; it was a massive failure in human decision-making. When the investigators listened to the cockpit voice recorder, it was clear that McBroom had attempted to keep track of everything by himself. He did not take advantage of the support offered by his crew and was so intent on solving the landing gear problem that he was not listening to them. Consistent with the cockpit culture of the time, the captain was the expert. Crew members were merely instruments for executing the captain's commands. In this culture, everyone understood you don't challenge the captain. You did what you were told and kept your mouth shut. All pilots understood the two unwritten rules of the cockpit. Rule #1: The captain is always right. Rule #2: If the captain is wrong, see Rule #1.[17]

Nevertheless, these two unwritten rules resulted in too many crashes. An analysis of aviation accidents in the 1970s showed that poor human decision-making enabled by an autocratic pilot culture resulted in needless crashes. While the captains were experts, they weren't infallible, and they were capable of senseless errors. Something had to be done. That something was called Crew Resource Management (CRM), and it would forever change the aviation industry for the better.

In 1981, United Airlines trained every one of its pilots in CRM. The training emphasized that, in a crisis, the crew members are a team. While the captain is the leader, he or she is not a dictator. They were taught how to quickly distribute tasks, and everyone was encouraged to speak up. The expectation was clear: Regardless of your rank or experience, if you see something, say something. In other words, it was the failure to speak up rather than speaking up that could lead to disciplinary action.

The pilots were videotaped in simulators as part of the training process to reinforce the new behavioral expectations. The story is told that when one crew was reviewing the training tape, a captain, seeing how others saw him for the first time, asked the instructor to stop the tape. He turned to his crewmates and asked, "Am I really like that?" When they replied yes, he said, "How can you work with me?" He knew he needed to change the way he managed his crews.

Today, CRM is the cultural norm across all airlines. Pilots understand that speaking up is not just a right, but an obligation, and no one has the authority to silence another team member. They don't defer to the thinking of the captain. They understand that the laws of physics have no regard for the egos and opinions of experts overly invested in their own thinking. Instead, they blend their collective intelligence by working as a team, and these teams don't filter data to fit their theories; they adapt their theories to fit the facts. By shifting to a new team-based management mindset that's focused on asking the right questions and forging a shared understanding of how to handle stressful, complex problems, these teams have greatly improved decision-making in the cockpit, as evidenced by the outstanding safety record of the commercial aviation industry in recent decades.

A Centuries-Old Mindset

Just as pilots needed to adopt a new mindset to improve their decision-making, today's business leaders are being challenged to think differently about how they do the business of business. That's because the advent of a new socioeconomic era changes our world and the way we see the world, as we learned when we transitioned from the Agrarian Age to the Industrial Age

Before the Industrial Revolution, the home was also the workplace where farmers and craftsmen toiled together with their spouses and children. During the Agrarian Age, life on the farm was defined by the dominant metaphor of its time—the land. Everyday language, through stories and parables, cultivated a mindset where life and work were viewed as part of the cycle of the seasons, and the job of the farmer was to understand and respect nature's laws and its sometimes unpredictable ways. For the farmer, work was about planting and harvesting, and responsibility was about aligning with and respecting the land. Farmers had no notion that work was about taking charge or being in control. They were very clear that the laws of nature were in command.

The Industrial Age radically altered society's mindset, with the machine replacing the land as the dominant metaphor defining social life. As the workers moved into the factories, work was no longer about tilling the land. It was now about running and making machines. It wasn't long before the world was viewed through the prism of the new machine mindset, where workers were viewed as parts of the factory and where their primary value was running the factory's machines efficiently to leverage the power of mass production. As this mindset took hold, managers viewed themselves as corporate machine operators who could control the machines and their people through their superior skills and intelligence.

Mindsets are born from assumptions that are often true when first formulated. As the assumptions continually verify themselves through repeated successes, they become unquestioned and eventually fade into the background, often becoming unconscious. What remains is the accepted ways of thinking and acting and everyone's understanding that that's just the way it is. For well over a century, the machine mindset has dominated corporate management because, in its day, it was an idea whose time had come. Throughout the twentieth century, centralized production design created and expanded markets; authoritative take-charge managers achieved results, and monitoring all the tasks assured the accomplishment of activities. Nevertheless, as the management author Gary Hamel keenly observes, "Most of the essential tools and techniques of modern management were invented by individuals born in the 19th century, not long after the end of the American Civil War."[18]

Command-and-control management thrived throughout the twentieth century for many reasons. The machine mindset had become socialized across society as the mass production of machines radically transformed how people worked. Bosses were accepted as essential for assuring work proceeded as planned, and giving them authority to direct the work of large numbers was highly successful in efficiently producing affordable goods. Command-and-control management was generally accepted because it worked so well. Despite its shortcomings, how could anyone argue with its success? Thus, the hierarchical management model, with its mechanistic, linear thinking and propensity for planning and control, has become so pervasive that most people assume that there are no other alternatives, whether they like it or not. That is the power of a mindset.

Despite all their rhetoric today about empowerment and employee involvement, managers continue to lead by being in charge. Just like airline captains before CRM, they believe that is their job—and not to do so would be irresponsible. Until recently, the reason why the vast majority of managers lead by command and control, even though no one likes it, is because we see the world through the lens of the machine mindset. And from this perspective, that's just the way it is.

But is it? Just as the Industrial Age radically changed the thinking of the Agrarian Age, there are strong indications that the Digital Age and its new dominant metaphor, the network, are spawning a new mindset to enable better and more intelligent decision-making. The land mindset did not last forever, and neither will the machine mindset.

The greatest personal challenge for traditional business leaders today is coming to terms with the reality that top-down hierarchical management is an idea whose time has passed. Once they understand this, business leaders will be ready to adopt a radically different paradigm that sees the world not as a machine but as a network. In the next chapter, we will begin to explore the network mindset and its new ways of thinking and acting. However, before you turn the page, be prepared because everything you have believed about the way we work and the work we do is about to change dramatically.

3

DISCOVERING THE
POWER OF NETWORKS

I n his prescient book, *The Seventh Sense: Power, Fortune, and Survival in the Age of Networks*, Joshua Cooper Ramo relates the story of one the most closely guarded secrets during the early years of the Cold War: If the Soviet Union had engaged in a nuclear first strike, it was highly likely the United States would have been unable to respond. That's because the American field officers and their commanders in Washington would have had no way to communicate with each other. Consistent with the technology at the time, the American radio and telephone systems were highly centralized, which made them highly vulnerable. One of the key structural problems of centralized systems is that each regional center has the potential to become a single point of failure that can disrupt the entire system, as often happens when air traffic across a nation is snarled because of unexpected weather at a major hub.

Fortunately, this national security vulnerability was corrected with an innovative solution: the distributed network. Recognizing the urgency of this challenge, Paul Baran, who was with the joint venture between the US Air Force and the Douglas Aircraft Company known as RAND, devised a way of building messaging systems without any central hubs. Each message would be able to find its path from point A to point B. Thus, if any part of the system was disrupted, the remaining pathways in the network could resiliently adapt to route all the traffic in the system with minimal disruption.

In solving this critical military problem, Baran recognized that central control is the fatal flaw in the hierarchical organization model. He eliminated this flaw by designing a model in which central control was simply not possible. In his new model, connectivity—not control—provided the source of power for solving problems and getting things done.

Baran's revolutionary insight about transforming how power worked is the organizational equivalent of Einstein's discovery of relativity. As Einstein's discoveries forever changed how we understand the universe, Baran's insights have the potential to forever change how we organize the world. However, for that to happen, we will need to become very familiar with the dynamics of how networks work, and that's a problem because, as Ramo notes, "We are at an extremely primitive point in our understanding of networks."[1] This lack of understanding was a reality that I faced a few years ago when I was suddenly confronted with a problem that could only be solved by first learning how networks work.

WE'RE A NETWORK, NOT A HIERARCHY

In the spring of 1998, I was asked to lead the Blue Cross Blue Shield Federal Employee Program (FEP) operations, the world's largest privately underwritten health insurance arrangement. In the mid-1990s, FEP covered more than 3.7 million US federal employees and their families, which represented 43 percent of the available market among the federal workforce. This was significantly lower than the 62 percent market share that FEP held in the mid-1970s when, due to the need to significantly raise rates to cover rising benefit expenses, FEP's market share plummeted to 39 percent in two years. Despite the introduction of a new product option as a recovery strategy, over twenty years, FEP only recovered a mere four points of the lost market share and struggled operationally and financially. Our challenge was clear: End two decades of low performance and restore FEP to a solid growth position.

As we assessed what needed to be done differently, an early insight turned out to be the linchpin that would generate a very successful turnaround: We're a network, not a hierarchy. So, we have to learn how to lead a network.

Blue Cross Blue Shield is not your typical business organization. It's a confederation of the separate Blue Cross Blue Shield companies distributed across the United States. FEP is a joint venture of all the Blue Cross Blue Shield organizations whose purpose is to deliver a seamless health insurance product in the federal employee marketplace, which includes scores of insurance options in this unique, individual choice market. The challenge for the Blues was to achieve seamlessness across the thirty-nine separate companies participating in this joint venture. Our inability to successfully coordinate at the level we needed across this large number of organizations clearly contributed to our performance woes.

Up to this point, our basic management model was an adaptation of the common top-down, hierarchical, command-and-control structure. Although there were attempts at building consensus before taking action, agreement generally eluded us as these thirty-nine organizations would often put their local interests ahead of the welfare of the overall program. Without a workable consensus, the administrative office in Washington, DC would formulate top-down directives that were not always well-received by the various participating Blues. Instead of compliant implementation, many of the Blues pushed back, making it clear they didn't report to the administrative offices in Washington. Consequently, far too much of our interaction was focused on fruitless discussions about who was in charge. Clearly, this was not a formula for operational excellence.

As we began the work of learning how to effectively lead a network, we realized we were in unchartered waters. The body of management knowledge in which we had all been trained—in both academic business schools and commercial management courses— was premised on the assumption that business organizations are hierarchically structured. In the commercial courses, in particular, the common orientation focused on training managers to use their in-charge power more humanely. Because one of the distinguishing characteristics of networks, especially distributed networks, is that the exercise of power has more to do with being connected than being in charge, most of our traditional leadership training was of little use in informing us about what was needed to lead a network. If we were going to succeed in making this leadership shift, we needed to become trailblazers.

No-Debate Meetings

Our first order of business on our trailblazing leadership journey was to find a way to accomplish what had evaded us for two decades in two days: a workable consensus among the joint venture partners. Achieving this ambitious goal meant we needed to radically transform our meetings, which, up to this point, were often endless debates repeatedly covering the same basic agenda without reaching any mutually acceptable conclusions.

Our meetings often felt like highjack experiences where three or four people took control of the room by dominating the discussion, arguing past each other, and no one making any attempt to truly understand different points of view. Instead of finding common ground, these dominators became more entrenched in their vested interests. The dominators were not necessarily the most thoughtful people in the room but were usually more extroverted. This was often troublesome because when these extroverted dominators had effectively accomplished the meeting highjack, the thoughtful introverts would often shut down and become silent. When the voices of the most thoughtful are effectively squelched, there's little hope of achieving a workable consensus. If we were to change the quality of our meetings, we had to stop the dominator debates. We needed to design a "no debate" format.

With this picture in mind, we began the task of designing a very different kind of meeting. Instead of setting up the room in the usual form of a U-shaped table, the forty participants would be seated at five round tables. Rather than serving as the chairman overseeing a committee-style meeting, the session leader would act as a facilitator leading the group through a series of interactive exercises. Instead of a schedule of meeting agenda topics, the focus of the facilitated session would be three to four concrete action objectives to motivate the group toward getting things done. Most importantly, there would be no debate in the large group forum. Debate would happen in the small group sessions where the influence of the dominators would be diffused, and the introverts would be more comfortable coming forward with their ideas.

A key discipline that turned out to be one of the most transformative attributes of our new meeting format was the practice of clarifying questions. When the small groups reported the results of their discussions to the large group forum, the participants were restricted to clarifying questions only. All they could do was ask questions to better understand the point of view of the presenting group. They could not agree, disagree, or present another point of view. This discipline of clarifying questions accomplished two things. First, it favored understanding over advocacy in the presentation of differing ideas. Second, it inhibited the fruitless debate that had been the albatross of our traditional meeting format.

Another key discipline was the practice of dot voting. When the small group reports were completed, we consolidated the items identified by each group into a mutually exclusive list. We then gave each participant strips of four stick-on dots that they could apply to indicate which items were most important to handling the problem we were attempting to solve. Typically, the results of the voting identified a clear number of items, usually four, that everyone agreed would work to solve the issue.

Our no-debate meetings exceeded our wildest expectations. We suddenly had a meeting format that could reliably and consistently accomplish a workable consensus among the many disparate partners in our business alliance. This newfound ability to rapidly create consensus was a prime contributor to turning the business around. Within two years, we had gained as much enrollment as we had realized over the previous two decades, and over the ensuing years, we gained back all the lost enrollment and more. This was possible because we had effectively learned how to lead a network.

Discovering Collective Intelligence

The new meeting format was an immediate hit with the early participants. In the evaluations of the initial sessions, the two most frequent comments were, "I can't believe how much we accomplished in so short an amount of time," and "No single one of us could have ever come up with the solutions we created as a group." While the first comment validated a clear objective we had in mind when we created these no-debate meetings, the second comment reflected the emergence of a fortunate, unintended consequence that would be the most powerful dynamic of our new meeting format. We had serendipitously discovered a way to rapidly aggregate the group's collective intelligence. In designing a no-debate meeting, we created a collective intelligence workshop, which is how this innovative meeting format is known today. Once we recognized this unexpected phenomenon, we could leverage this fortunate discovery into a powerful management tool.

Over the next decade, as we witnessed our business's remarkable turnaround and growth, we learned that the emergence of collective intelligence in our new meeting format was not an accident but a natural and inevitable property of a well-constructed network. That's because, while top-down hierarchies are designed to leverage the individual intelligence of the leaders at the top of the organization, networks are inclined to leverage the collective intelligence of all the participants in the peer-to-peer structure.

The capacity to rapidly aggregate collective intelligence is the great organizational game-changer. However, it can be hard for people who are used to leading by control to appreciate the power of collective wisdom. As James Surowiecki, the author of *The Wisdom of Crowds,* notes, "One of the striking things about the wisdom of crowds is that even though its effects are all around us, it's easy to miss, and, even when it's seen, it can be hard to accept."[2]

The Wisdom of Crowds

In his seminal book, Surowiecki provides numerous examples where, under the right conditions, distributed groups are highly intelligent and consistently outperform even the smartest individuals among them. He describes how the sports bookmakers at the Mirage assure the profitability of betting operations at the Las Vegas hotel by relying on the collective judgments of the gamblers to set the betting lines and how Linus Torvalds defied logic by introducing the phenomenon that has come to be known as crowdsourcing to build the highly successful Linux operating system. Surowiecki also recounts how Google, a late entry into a crowded field of upstarts, established quick dominance of the search engine market when a pair of Stanford graduate students discovered a way to use the collective intelligence of the users to rank the pages.

Despite these compelling examples, tapping into the wisdom of the crowd is more the exception than the rule. Perhaps that's because accessing collective intelligence is not as easy as it may appear. Many leaders feel that they are tapping into this resource by gathering people with different perspectives and managing a spirited discussion among multiple points of view before making an executive decision. While they may be well-intentioned, this is not how collective intelligence works.

Surowiecki specifies four conditions that are necessary to access the wisdom of the crowd:

- *Diversity of opinion*: Having different perspectives—even eccentric notions—broadens the available information, provides the capacity for evolving ideas, makes it easier for individuals to be candid, and protects against the negative dynamics of shortsighted groupthink.

- *Independent thinking*: Everyone is free to express his or her opinions without editing and without any pressure to conform to the beliefs of others in the group. Surowiecki points out that "paradoxically, the best way for a group to be smart is for each person in it to think and act as independently as possible."[3]

- *Local knowledge*: To truly access collective intelligence, the group must be able to draw upon specialized and localized knowledge because the closer a person is to the problem or the customer, the more likely he or she is to make a meaningful contribution.
- *Aggregation mechanisms*: A distributed system can only produce genuinely intelligent results if there are processes or algorithms for integrating the content of everyone's observations and opinions.

Without all four conditions, accessing collective intelligence is not possible. That is why the leader who gathers different perspectives into a lively discussion is not tapping into the group's collective wisdom. Although he or she may have access to multiple perspectives and input from those with extensive local knowledge, organizational politics are likely to interfere with independent thinking. And when the leader is processing the consolidation of the information, there is clearly no aggregation mechanism.

The FEP collective intelligence workshops were effective because they incorporated all four conditions. By including forty people from all levels, disciplines, and perspectives across our network, we assured diversity of opinion and local knowledge. Discussing issues at small group tables and using dot voting encouraged independent thinking. Dot voting also provided an aggregation mechanism that balanced all voices and allowed the group's collective intelligence to emerge.

STRUCTURAL VALUE PREFERENCES

FEP's use of a radically different management model to lead a business turnaround and Baran's solution to solving a major security issue are two examples of the power of networks. In learning how to lead the FEP network, we discovered that *hierarchies and networks are not equal alternative structures*. Networks tend to outperform hierarchies by a wide margin. Like others who have embraced this radically different model, we made a dramatic leap in performance because we built our organization around a distinct set of values that are very different from the practices of traditional management.

In designing the work of large numbers of people, the leaders of organizations need to make a series of structural value preferences among the five sets of paradoxical values presented in Figure 3-1.

Figure 3-1. Structural Value Preferences

Collective Intelligence **vs.** Elite Intelligence

Iterative Discovery **vs.** Central Planning

Synergistic Power **vs.** Coercive Power

Diversity of Opinion **vs.** Uniformity of Thought

Agreement **vs.** Compliance

In approaching these preferences, it's important to note that these are not either/or choices. Instead, leaders are looking to balance two paradoxical values with a clear preference for one value over the other. To understand how these preferences work, let's borrow an analogy from the field of psychology.

One of the most insightful contributions to understanding human development is Erik Erikson's Stages of Psychosocial Development, which postulates that individuals, throughout their lives, move through a progression of eight psychosocial stages to reach their full development.[4] Each stage's essential work is resolving the tension between two paradoxical values. For example, in the first stage, an individual needs to balance the two values of Basic Trust vs. Basic Mistrust. While it is obvious that trust is the preferred value in developing a healthy personality, there are times when mistrust is appropriate. That's why a person who is always trusting is often regarded as a "Pollyanna."

On the other hand, one who is always mistrusting is considered paranoid. The important point is that the exclusive use of either value is generally problematic. Thus, the healthy person develops a sense of both trust and mistrust, but not necessarily in equal parts. In striking a balance between the two values, the psychologically fit clearly prefers trust over mistrust. While they usually lead with trust, they are savvy enough to know when to mistrust. On the other hand, an unhealthy personality leads with mistrust, making it difficult to build healthy relationships.

The dynamics of this psychological model are analogous to the development of organizations, except that all the preferences are built into the initial organizational design rather than in a series of stages. However, like Erikson's model, the value choices are not equivalent when building a healthy organization.

Since their inception well over a century ago, public and private organizations have clearly preferred the values on the right in Figure 3-1 over those on the left, which explains why the vast majority of organizations are designed as hierarchical bureaucracies. These top-down structures assume the smartest organizations are the ones that can effectively leverage the intelligence of their smartest individuals. Accordingly, strategy is the responsibility of the elite few, which is discerned through central planning and executed by endowing managers with command-and-control authority to assure uniformity of thought and compliance. These preferences, clearly consistent with Frederick Taylor's scientific management, became so enculturated throughout the twentieth century that business leaders continue to assume the top-down, centralized hierarchy is the only way large organizations can be managed, and there are no alternatives.

The problem with bureaucracies is that by leveraging the individual intelligence of the elite experts, they kill the human spirit of the many, which may explain why Gallup's worker engagement surveys consistently find that only about a third of employees are actively engaged in their work, a clear signal that most organizations are not healthy workplaces. This is problematic because unhealthy workplaces kill not only the human spirit, but also the capacity for innovation. This is further compounded by the reality that experts are rarely innovators. Experts are highly knowledgeable about the way things have been done in the past and are often heavily invested in the status quo. This tendency often causes experts to be blind to future possibilities that may challenge conventional ways, as we saw in Chapter 2 when John Antioco, Blockbuster's CEO, turned down the opportunity to buy Netflix, dismissing the internet as completely overblown.

This blindness is an inherent organizational design flaw that can be fatal when businesses need to be highly competent at innovation. This flaw is a product of the fundamental design principle that shapes the top-down, hierarchical organizational model: *Trust authority.* Hierarchies ascribe authority to the elite few who perform two specific roles—bosses and experts—to bring order to the workflow of large numbers of people. Bosses are given command-and-control authority to ensure management directives are carried out, and experts are often the exclusive source of intelligence within organizations. In some instances, these are two different sets of people; in other instances, these roles can reside with the same person. Top-down hierarchies are designed to amplify the voices of these two trusted authoritative roles.

Unfortunately, one consequence of relying on the intelligence of the elite few to guide decision-making is that organizations limit their intelligence. In stable times, this flaw may be livable, but in rapidly changing times, as we learned with Blockbuster, this flaw can be fatal.

When focused on making organizations as efficient as machines, it is easy to lose sight of the fact that humans are not machines, and individuals—even highly intelligent individuals—are not exempt from cognitive biases. These cognitive biases can lead to faulty decision-making and senseless errors, as with Captain McBroom on United Flight 173, which we also discussed in Chapter 2.

When the guiding design principle of organizations is to trust authority and when people are expected to do what they're told, it is easy to see how elite intelligence, coercive power, central planning, uniformity of thought, and compliance are the clear preferences that shape the thinking inside organizations and define the work experience. Everyone is expected to get on board with the thinking of the elite few and comply with the plan. Thus, hierarchical management's prime focus is control, especially controlling people.

Thinking Differently

At FEP, we recognized we had to change and learn how to lead a network because we accepted the reality that continued attempts to control people in thirty-nine separate organizations would be futile. We realized we had to think differently and learn how to manage by consensus. In making this transformation, we chose the values on the left of Figure 3-1 as our preferences for designing a very different management model. The design principle of our new approach was a sharp departure from traditional management: *Nobody is smarter than everybody*. Living out this model, we became skilled at aggregating and leveraging our collective intelligence. Accordingly, we welcomed diversity of opinion and developed tools and practices to rapidly integrate divergent views into innovative solutions that no single person—no matter how intelligent—could devise.

Because of our commitment to diversity of opinion, we became a far more intelligent organization that was no longer bound by the limits of individual cognitive biases. By encouraging the expression of divergent points of view and using sophisticated facilitation tools to uncover common ground and create higher-level, convergent solutions, we could move beyond the rancor that had handicapped us for so many years. Instead, we found a way to consistently reach unanimous agreements that rendered the need for compliance meaningless. We learned that the right action is more likely to emerge from an iterative discovery discipline than fixed central planning. We also learned when you become proficient at leading networks, you understand why management by agreement is far more productive than management by compliance. When an organization is designed around the principle that all voices matter and becomes skilled at creating intelligence that no single individual could ever accomplish, it amplifies the human connectivity that is an essential ingredient for innovation. This enables an organization that's built to last because the capacity to adapt to change is built into its organizational DNA.

A memorable example of how valuing everyone's voice and thinking differently created a deep understanding of how to solve a business problem illustrates the incredible power of collective intelligence. In one of FEP's early collective intelligence workshops, I facilitated forty people who had spent several hours in a series of small group discussions, large group exercises, and dot voting to identify the key actions needed to solve a nagging issue. It appeared that we had reached an acceptable consensus with the participants. As I looked over the group, however, I sensed that one person was not entirely comfortable with the group's solution. I turned to that person and shared my observation. I noted that if she had a different preference for how to solve the issue but felt the group's solution would work, it would make sense to go along. However, if she felt the solution the group was considering would not work and could exacerbate our problem, I told her that she had a responsibility to share her concerns. We needed to listen to what she had to say because she might be seeing something the rest of us had missed. She stood up and told the group she was very uncomfortable with the approach we were contemplating. She expressed her concerns and engaged in a thoughtful dialogue with the group. She convinced them we needed to take a radically different course of action to truly solve the issue. She did see something the rest of us didn't, and by making it safe to express her dissent, the group arrived at a more intelligent solution.

This example demonstrates two important observations about collective intelligence and networks. The first is collective intelligence is not a simple matter of majority rules. Majorities can sometimes silence the voices of those who think differently, weakening or eliminating two of the four conditions necessary for collective intelligence: diversity of opinion and independent thinking. It isn't only individual autocrats who can abuse coercive power; majorities that extinguish the voices of minorities are also capable of political coercion. Unlike hierarchies, the goal of networks is agreement, not compliance.

The second observation is that when one individual convinces an entire group to radically shift course, we are still leveraging the collective intelligence of the group. That's because the woman in our example did not have the power to command or manipulate the other participants to accept her thinking. As is the norm in networks, everyone else in the group maintained their right to think independently. Ultimately, everyone freely agreed to the change in the group's solution, and the four conditions were met. In this example, the aggregation mechanism was the genuine dialogue that resulted in a highly intelligent solution.

As we became more familiar with the dynamics of how networks worked, we realized the enablers of our success were a collection of unusual properties that were natural attributes of the design principle that nobody is smarter than everybody. What makes collective intelligence such a powerful asset is that it is extraordinarily intelligent, incredibly fast, consistently unbiased, and inherently altruistic.

EXTRAORDINARILY INTELLIGENT

In the traditional organization, debates are the typical means for processing human information. Decision makers often bring people together who hold different points of view in meetings where various parties engage in vigorous discussions to persuade the decision maker to their way of thinking. When debates are successful, the result is often a compromise, which is usually some form of a least common denominator solution. How often have we heard it said that a sign of an effective compromise is that everybody gets something and everyone feels a little pain? In other words, a compromise is often a combination of both win-win and lose-lose. In a world dominated by hierarchical structures, we have come to accept that least-common-denominator solutions are often the best we can do.

Our collective intelligence workshops, however, rarely produced least-common-denominator solutions. Instead, they typically resulted in highly intelligent actions that were the best possible solutions we could devise. That's why so many participants felt we were accomplishing results that no one of us could ever achieve on our own. These higher-order solutions typically were true win-win victories, which is why we consistently achieved unanimous consensus among the participants in these sessions.

In achieving optimal solutions where no one loses, and everybody wins, we eliminated the hidden agenda that often results in surreptitious pushback and sometimes outright sabotage. To our surprise, we discovered that our extraordinarily intelligent solutions were easily and immediately understood by the many people in our network who were not participants in the session. This is what happens when a solution is a true win-win, and nobody loses. These highly intelligent solutions enabled an extraordinary level of synergy among the many distributed participants in our network and were prime drivers behind the successful turnaround of our business.

INCREDIBLY FAST

In addition to being extraordinarily intelligent, the results that emerged in our collective intelligence workshops happened incredibly fast. When debates are the primary vehicle for processing human information, the pathway to knowledge and effective action is often long and arduous, as had been the case in FEP. In many instances, the debates had become endless and went on for months or even years without meaningful resolution. However, when we transformed our meetings into collective intelligence sessions, we were pleasantly surprised at how consistently we could accomplish highly effective solutions in a mere matter of hours. We discovered that networks, with their propensity for collective intelligence, are far faster pathways to knowledge. A closer examination of the different pathways of debates and collective intelligence workshops explains why this is so.

In debates, the pathway to knowledge is through the individual brains of everyone involved in the meeting. That's why there is so much discussion. Individuals present their ideas and argue their perspectives through point and counterpoint. The fundamental dynamic at work in debates is persuasion, with the goal that, after all points of view have been thoroughly vetted, either one person's thinking or a combination of different points of view will be accepted by most individuals in the meeting. While this goal is well intended, it is rarely achieved. Often, the individuals do not accomplish mutual closure, and the issue is left to be discussed another day. If there is an immediate need to act, a single decision-maker will issue a directive based on his or her best understanding. Whether the issue is mutually resolved, left for another day, or decided by executive fiat, the pathway to knowledge in debates is a function of the individual brain. If action is taken, it's because either all the individual brains agree or one individual brain has made a decision for the group.

Collective intelligence is a faster pathway to knowledge because it is not subject to the limitations of the individual brain or the need to influence the thinking of various individuals to reach closure. Collective intelligence shifts the context of the gathering from a collection of separate individual brains to a network of interconnected brains, which means there is often no need for debate because it's the emergence of collective thinking rather than the persuasion of individual thinking that is the key dynamic operating on this pathway. This means—as counterintuitive as it may seem—it is possible, through the emergent nature of collective intelligence, to reach meaningful closure on the right action to deal with difficult and complex issues without a single word of discussion. We see this repeatedly in our collective intelligence workshops, where groups of forty or more people generate more than 200 ideas and, through two rounds of dot voting, will unanimously arrive at the top four ideas that will serve as the framework for effective action—and they accomplish this in less than an hour. Because we are tapping into the network of brains rather than trying to influence individuals one brain at a time, we can achieve fast and real closure.

Consistently Unbiased

One of the primary reasons we had so much difficulty in our prior attempts to reach a consensus among the thirty-nine companies in our business alliance was that the participants were heavily focused on doing what was in the best interest of their particular organizations. Very often, what was in the best interest of one company was at odds with the interests of other organizations in the alliance. This meant that many participants came to our meetings with strong biases that were clear impediments to achieving integrated solutions that would be acceptable to all the companies.

One of the most surprising outcomes of the collective intelligence workshops was how using this innovative meeting format reliably delivered solutions that moved us past the individual biases of the participants. While we had hoped these no-debate workshops would accelerate our ability to reach a workable consensus, we were amazed at how consistently the sessions resulted in unanimous consensus among the forty to fifty workshop participants. We had somehow discovered a way to move past the individual biases of the participants and craft unbiased solutions that preserved what was most important to everyone. This happens when a meeting process is designed to produce higher-order solutions rather than the least-common-denominator compromises typical of debates.

As we reflected on the workings of this newfound competency, we noticed that the emergent solutions tended to have four or five key elements. Usually, there was an element critical to one faction in the group, an apparently contradictory element important to another faction with an opposing point of view, and two or three elements that helped bridge the apparently opposing elements such that the set of elements taken as a whole was acceptable to all the stakeholders in the workshops. The ability to achieve unbiased solutions while preserving the particular interests of opposing factions is one of the most powerful attributes of collective intelligence.

Inherently Altruistic

Another powerful attribute is that collective intelligence tends to be inherently altruistic. Because the unbiased solutions that emerge from successfully aggregating collective intelligence blend apparently opposing elements into workable action, there is no longer a need for differing factions to compete with or, worse, demonize each other. Instead, all participants are poised to accomplish common action that benefits both the overall network and the individual contributors. This benevolence enables a high level of collaboration within the distributed peer-to-peer network that is rarely, if ever, achieved in centralized top-down hierarchies. This high level of collaboration became the foundational context that sustained the remarkable turnaround of FEP.

This final attribute is of particular importance to our world today as we stand on the threshold of the development of artificial intelligence (AI). Many are concerned AI could pose a threat to humanity as the intelligence of AI outpaces human intelligence. This concern reflects an assumption that AI will be a collection of individual agents that will behave and act as do individual human agents today, with similar strengths, weaknesses, and biases, and that AI agents will use their superior intelligence to control as much as of their world as they can, including the humans with whom they compete. However, it doesn't have to be this way. If artificial intelligence platforms are built as collective intelligence systems, AI will likely be extraordinarily intelligent, incredibly fast, consistently unbiased, and, most importantly, inherently altruistic. These powerful, altruistic, collective intelligence systems will be far more likely to enhance rather than compete with humanity.

POWERFUL AND TIMELY LESSONS

It is often said that necessity is the mother of invention. This was certainly true in our case at FEP as we engaged in our trailblazing journey to learn how to lead a network. We had greatly expanded our understanding of how networks work and had learned, as Paul Baran did, that well-designed distributed networks are far more powerful systems than centralized hierarchies.

We were eager to share our experiences with others in our larger company but were surprised by the reactions of our colleagues. Despite the obvious success of our business unit and our willingness to share what we had learned about leading networks, the leaders of other units were not interested in adopting our innovative organizational practices. Perhaps the greatest impediment was the fear of losing personal control that network leaders must embrace for a peer-to-peer management architecture to work. When power is about being connected rather than being in charge, personal control over the work of large numbers of people in an organization becomes meaningless. What is important is creating a practical platform where all within an organization can effectively leverage their collective intelligence in the service of customers. This is the guiding dynamic that makes Linux, the popular open-source software operating system, so powerful.

The management irony is that, often, the best way for leaders to ensure their organizations remain under control is for them to give up the notion that they can personally control the work of others. The enablement of effective self-organization, a natural attribute of peer-to-peer networks, is the hallmark of a well-controlled twenty-first-century organization. Conversely, when leaders insist on maintaining tight control over everything happening within their businesses, they often leave companies spinning out of control in their wake.

Legacy business leaders underestimate the inherent capabilities of self-organization because they can't comprehend how anything will work if no one is in charge, despite the immense success of self-organized enterprises such as Linux, Wikipedia, and, more recently, Bitcoin. They pass these examples off as aberrations rather than recognizing them as harbingers. Perhaps what is most troubling is that most legacy leaders have little or no experience in the abundant capacity of collective intelligence. This is because our education systems reinforce a mindset that believes intelligence is fundamentally an attribute of the individual.

The Power of Mindsets

Education is one of the primary ways we become socialized into society. The socialization process is how we generally form mindsets that guide how we make sense of the world around us. Mindsets are pathways to understanding how the world works. They integrate the common assumptions, values, and beliefs that shape ways of thinking and acting among large groups of people. Mindsets are useful social tools for processing the uncertainty and ambiguity around us so we can have a sense of a shared reality. This shared reality becomes the context in which we develop the ideas, concepts, and perceptions that become the mental models for engaging each other in social relationships.

While mental models help us make sense of the world around us, over time, mindsets can become so strongly held that we collectively become unaware that mindsets are also mental boundaries that limit and constrain our thinking in ways we fail to recognize. In other words, mindsets shape what we collectively see and, equally important, what we collectively don't see. When education systems and other social institutions reinforce the notion that human intelligence is primarily an individual attribute, power belongs to those in charge, and things get accomplished when they are effectively controlled, people's mindsets are predisposed to hierarchical ways of thinking and acting. This explains why so many people, especially those born and raised before the digital revolution, fail to recognize and understand the unique dynamics of networks. Understanding how networks work requires proactively adopting a new mindset, and that can be a difficult task as it often means discarding deeply held assumptions and beliefs.

This is worrisome because many business, political, and organizational leaders feel no incentive to improve their understanding of networks. In fact, they are likely incentivized to resist rebalancing the structural value preferences in Figure 3-1 to favor those on the left side of the chart. Unlike Einstein's theories, which had little practical effect on how people went about living their day-to-day lives, embracing Baran's architectural innovation is likely to be perceived as a clear and present danger to those who hold the reins of power. As noted above, in networks, power belongs to the connected. This means those in charge will no longer be in charge, which can feel very threatening for legacy leaders.

Though we can expect legions of leaders to resist mightily, their resistance will clearly be futile because, as Ramo notes, "The essence of what Baran discovered reveals that certain types of networks, once they take a grip on our world, represent an irreversible transition."[5] There's no going back from Wikipedia to Britannica, Instagram to Kodak, or Netflix to Blockbuster. Each of these examples is an illustration of a power shift from those in charge to those who were connected, and despite whatever resistance the leaders of the displaced iconic companies might have attempted, in the end, they were ultimately powerless. Yet, despite these compelling examples, legacy leaders and most of us fail to recognize the significance of this power shift precisely because we stubbornly hold onto a mindset that insists the machine is the most effective metaphor to explain how the world works. That is why most of us have little or no understanding of the workings of networks.

One of the consequences of the digital revolution is a digital divide that pits the forces of hierarchies against the momentum of networks. While this struggle will play out—most likely chaotically—over the next decade, the outcome is fairly certain. The transition is indeed irreversible because hierarchies amplifying the individual intelligence of an elite few, as we've already seen in these first decades of the digital revolution, are no match against networks that can rapidly leverage human and artificial collective intelligence.

Rapidly increasing our understanding of how networks work and how to lead them is the most important leadership challenge of our day. Leaders can no longer afford to build centralized organizations where supervisors with the legitimate authority to kill good ideas or keep bad ideas alive become legions of single points of failure. If leaders are to build resilient organizations that have the wherewithal to rapidly adapt to disruptive change, their first task is to embrace a radically different way of understanding how the world works by learning how to build and lead highly effective distributed networks. It's not an option; it's an imperative.

4

BUILDING TEAMS OF LEADERS

Before the late nineteenth century, there were no bosses or subordinates. There were only workers. Before the Industrial Age, all business was small business, and the average size of the typical work group was four people.[1] Granted, all workers were not necessarily equal; there were mentors and apprentices. However, these were not permanent power arrangements but temporary learning relationships. In the businesses of the Agrarian Age, there were no supervisors who issued orders and expected compliance. A worker's authority was earned through professional competence rather than ascribed by the power of one's position. In the realm of business, the notion that authority is derived from one's role rather than one's practice only comes about with the emergence of the modern corporation and its need to organize the work of large numbers of people. Bosses are creations of the Industrial Age and are, thus, a relatively recent phenomenon in the history of work.

Shifting the locus of work from the farm and craftsman's shop to the assembly line created a need for overseers who would design the intricate processes of the factories, organize the workers' activities, and ensure that everything was working as designed. As overseers became the indispensable critical agents of budding corporate enterprises, it was generally accepted that, for these large organizations to leverage the efficiencies of the assembly line, overseers needed to have the authority to issue orders and the means to assure workers would comply. Accordingly, early Industrial Age enterprises met the new challenge of organizing large numbers of workers by arranging the corporation's activities into a hierarchical structure of supervisors and subordinates where the authority to command became the foundation for the practice of leadership. Thus, the central role in the command-and-control organization was and continues to be the boss.

In command-and-control organizations, leaders are bosses, and despite their relatively recent appearance in the world of work, most of us cannot conceive of an organization without bosses. Given the significant power and authority bestowed upon its leaders, the typical command-and-control organization seeks to promote the smartest and most effective individuals to executive positions. They rely on their native intelligence to set the direction for the company.

HEROIC LEADERS

In recruiting for key leadership positions, organizations invariably search for highly intelligent, dedicated, take-charge, charismatic individuals who can effectively persuade large numbers of people to their way of thinking. The archetype for executive leadership and the most common profile for recruiting top talent in command-and-control organizations is the heroic leader. These talented individuals are very enticing because they usually have track records of outstanding success. With their unique blend of native intelligence, business acumen, polished style, and persuasive personalities, heroic leaders can often accomplish the impossible when called upon to propel organizations from mediocrity to excellence. Their single-minded discipline and never-say-die attitudes can inspire and motivate large numbers of workers to improbable heights of success. The steady hand of a confident, take-charge, heroic leader at the helm in turbulent waters provides great comfort to board members navigating companies through difficult times. Command-and-control organizations firmly believe individual performers drive corporate success. And the consummate performer is the heroic leader.

One of the most visible and heralded performances of outstanding heroic leadership in recent years was the remarkable revival of the

Chrysler Corporation in the 1980s when Lee Iacocca assumed the top job. In the summer of 1978, Chrysler was in serious trouble and on the verge of going out of business. In a fortunate stroke of timing for the ailing automaker, Iacocca had recently been fired as president of the Ford Motor Company. Despite posting a $2 billion profit, Iacocca was let go after a clash of personalities with Henry Ford II over the future direction of product development at the number two carmaker. Iacocca's track record for producing consistent results, most notably the very popular Ford Mustang, was well known throughout the automotive industry. Chrysler was in desperate circumstances, and they needed a savior. So, they aggressively courted Iacocca, who agreed to become Chrysler's CEO in November 1978.

It didn't take long for Iacocca to realize that Chrysler was in far worse shape than he had anticipated. Ever the gifted problem solver and decision maker, Iacocca immediately took charge and put in place a three-pronged strategy to resurrect the dying corporation: 1) downsizing the company to reduce expenses and lower the break-even point, 2) securing congressional approval of $1.5 billion in federal loan guarantees, and 3) introducing the new product ideas that Ford had rejected. In a typical display of heroism, Iacocca galvanized Chrysler's workers by sharing the sacrifice and reducing his salary to $1.00 per year until the turnaround was complete.

Iacocca's strategic moves wildly exceeded the Chrysler board's expectations as the recovering automaker's new products, the K-cars and the very popular minivan, became instant hits with car buyers and quickly turned the company's fortunes around. In 1983, a full seven years ahead of schedule, Chrysler completely paid back its federally guaranteed loans. In 1984, the company posted annual profits of $2.4 billion, more than the previous sixty years combined.

Heroic leadership works, which explains why so many companies use the profile of the heroic leader to guide their searches when recruiting for executive talent. However, heroic leadership doesn't work all the time. Unfortunately, not all confident, take-charge, charismatic leaders are effective. In fact, there are probably as many failures among the bosses who fit this profile as there are successes.

Until recently, the missteps of heroic leaders have not been fatal because the relatively stable pace of change of the Industrial Age usually provided sufficient time for corporations to replace the failed executive with another more successful heroic leader.

However, while incredible turnarounds are possible and do happen for some heroic leaders for short periods, corporate greatness is about staying power and decades of continual success. Far too often, the company is so dependent on the heroic leader's dominant thinking and powerful personality that there is an enormous vacuum once the leader is gone.

Look at what happened to Chrysler after Iacocca retired. A series of poor management decisions and an unsuccessful merger with Daimler-Benz diminished many of the remarkable accomplishments of the 1980s. Unable to sustain itself after regaining its independence, Chrysler was forced into another merger—this time with Fiat—to avoid certain bankruptcy.

Great companies in the Digital Age will be those with the capacity to adapt to continually changing markets and the ability to periodically reinvent themselves. When the pace of change accelerates, greatness is more about smart organizations than smart individuals. The first step to building a great company is to embrace a radically different profile when recruiting leaders because few heroic leaders have the skills or the competencies to build smart organizations.

Great Leaders

In his bestselling book *Good to Great*, Jim Collins highlights the findings of his team's extensive research into the question of whether a good company can become a great company. To answer this question, Collins and his researchers painstakingly analyzed the business results of over 1,400 companies selected from the Fortune 500 list from 1965 to 1995. They methodically searched for companies that shared the following profile: "fifteen-year cumulative stock returns at or below the general stock market, punctuated by a transition point, then cumulative returns at least three times the market over the next fifteen years."[2] Their search identified eleven companies that met the criteria for good-to-great organizations. While they found this transition very rare—less than 1 percent of the companies analyzed made the leap—nevertheless, the empirical research revealed it is possible for a good company to become a great one. Unfortunately, this research also revealed that most good companies never become great, causing Collins to observe that perhaps "good is the enemy of great."[3]

As the research team began to dig deeply into the habits and practices of this select group of companies, they were surprised and unprepared for a universal and unusual observation that cut across all eleven organizations, regardless of industry. They found that every one of the subject companies shared a leadership style that defied conventional wisdom. The leaders of good-to-great companies, whom they eventually labeled "Level 5 leaders," consistently displayed a paradoxical blend of personal humility and professional will.[4] While willful behavior was anticipated, the pervasive consistency of humility among all good-to-great leaders caught the researchers off guard. Their behavior starkly contrasted the egotistical displays we have come to accept in traditional leaders. These great leaders were not your usual heroes.

Collins uses the very effective analogy of the window and the mirror to capture the essence of the unconventional behavior of great leaders. He notes that when things in the company are going well, Level 5 leaders "look out the window," crediting others or factors outside themselves for the company's success. However, when things go poorly, they "look in the mirror" and take full responsibility for their business circumstances. These individuals behave very differently from typical heroic leaders who often take credit for others' ideas in good times and are quick to find someone or something else to blame when times are tough.

The universal presence of unexpected humility across all these Level 5 leaders captivated the researchers who, despite Collins' insistence that they disregard the executives in their identification of good-to-great habits, passionately persisted in pushing back. They argued that the unusually consistent humility was a vital factor that could not be ignored. Ultimately, Collins acquiesced to the researchers not because of their passionate conviction but because the research supported the conclusion. Thus, the significance of identifying this unique blend of personal humility and professional will—and perhaps the most important contribution from Collins' breakthrough research—is that we now have an empirical alternative profile for highly effective leadership to consider when recruiting top talent.

The humility observed in these great leaders should not be confused with either weakness or meekness. These exceptional executives shared a fearless professional will to do whatever was in the best interests of their companies. They were highly capable of making tough choices to do the right thing. Although it may seem counterintuitive, the combination of humility and will enabled these great leaders to be far stronger and more effective than their heroic counterparts. While the strong egos of the heroes went into high gear in service of themselves in difficult times, the great leaders understood that not everything was about them, freeing them to focus the full force of their talents in service of their companies when needed most.

Great leaders don't assume they are the smartest people in the room, nor do they need to be. When facing difficult circumstances, their unique combination of humility and will becomes a potent source of courage for these great leaders to put aside any illusions and deal with reality on its terms. Their strength and power are firmly rooted in their capacity to bring together the best thinking and unique talents of everyone in service of the company. Thus, their effectiveness is not derived from a strong ego or their abilities to take charge and persuade or coerce others to their way of thinking but from a courageous sense of integrity that enables them to realistically assess themselves, their colleagues, and their circumstances to bring out the best in everyone, so together, they can make the best of their circumstances.

The profile of the great leader, as portrayed in Collins' description of Level 5 leaders, is very different from the common template used by most companies to recruit their top talent. As a result, most recruiters and hiring executives are unprepared to recognize the best executive talent, often turning away the very leaders who are most likely to build sustainable, smart organizations. Instead, they continue to recruit heroic leaders who are constrained by their deep-seated belief that they are far smarter and more capable than the people around them. Operating from this illusion, they are often overly focused on being right and demonstrating the full extent of their intelligence. Their inflated pride in their skills as problem solvers and decision makers often serves to diminish the talents of their supporting cast as they far too easily dismiss alternative opinions and consistently edit the thinking and contributions of their subordinates.

These behaviors often indicate narcissistic traits. This makes sense because narcissistic personalities are attracted to social roles that allow them to wield significant control and place them at the center of attention. Narcissistic leaders believe that the success or failure of the company is all about them. Unfortunately, most executive recruiters and hiring managers seem to share this misguided belief, which explains why there seems to be an overrepresentation of narcissistic personalities among corporate senior executives.

FROM CHESS MASTERS TO GARDENERS

The combination of personal humility and professional will that typifies Level 5 leaders allows them to more easily abandon yesterday's assumptions and embrace the realities of fast-changing times more effectively than leaders whose sense of professional identity is firmly rooted in their past accomplishments. The need to abandon conventional ways and embrace a new paradigm of leadership became a difference-maker for a military leader who suddenly found himself with a troubling conundrum: What do you do when you are leading the most highly trained and efficient military force in the world and find you are consistently failing to defeat a weaker enemy? That was the challenge General Stanley McChrystal faced when he took command of the Joint Special Operations Task Force in Iraq in 2003. While the general's army was organized into a highly efficient centralized hierarchy of thousands of disciplined soldiers, the Al Qaeda terrorists were using speed and adaptability to outmaneuver the troops by operating as a decentralized network of local units that could move quickly, strike brutishly, and become hidden in plain sight by blending into the local population. Al Qaeda was a different kind of enemy; defeating them would require different ways of thinking and acting.

McChrystal quickly recognized if his army was going to subdue the terrorists, he would have to solve the troops' adaptability problem. Because efficient practices are often barriers to adaptability, the general knew becoming more agile would mean abandoning centuries of conventional wisdom and adopting new rules for managing his troops. These new rules would be guided by a key principle that emerged as an observation from McChrystal's leadership team: *It takes a network to defeat a network.*[5]

In considering how to transform his troops into an adaptable network, McChrystal recognized that he would need to radically change his mental model about how organizations work. By virtue of his education at West Point and his experiences as a highly successful military officer, McChrystal was an expert in the practice of hierarchical command-and-control management. One of its core principles is the sharp separation of planning from execution, which in the military means the generals do the planning and the troops carry out their prescribed orders. The implicit assumption of top-down management is the notion that organizations are most effective when they are designed to leverage the individual intelligence of an elite few. This model also presumes that detailed planning by the elites can achieve predictable results. Thus, according to McChrystal, hierarchical leaders are trained to think like chess masters, using their talents and skills to exert control over their opponents.[6] In hierarchies, the power of an organization is a derivative of the skillful exercise of power by those in charge.

The network model reflects a very different set of organizing principles that assumes social systems work like organic ecosystems. In networks, power is a derivative of the strength of the connections among all the participants. Unlike hierarchies that leverage the intelligence of the elite few, effective networks can leverage the collective intelligence of the many and create a shared understanding across the organization. This shared understanding provides the wherewithal for participants to autonomously adapt to unpredictable circumstances. Accordingly, these highly distributed decentralized structures are impervious to the usual control tactics that are effective between two hierarchically structured enemies. Neutralizing an adversary's central command is not an option when the enemy is a decentralized network.

Transforming his organization into a superior network meant that McChrystal had to become a different kind of leader. In his words, he needed to stop playing chess and become a gardener.[7] He needed to shift his focus from moving pieces on a board to shaping an ecosystem. He accomplished this by structuring his troops into a collection of relatively autonomous teams, with select members from each team participating on intersecting teams to form a highly connected network that enabled a transparent shared understanding across the troops. Leveraging this shared understanding greatly increased the army's capacity to enhance their resource superiority with speed and adaptability.

A key element of this new networked architecture was incorporating a practice used at NASA that is known by the simple moniker "systems management."[8] In the early days of NASA, the agency experienced several embarrassing failures. For example, in November 1960, NASA's first unmanned test flight was a disaster as the launcher made it off the ground only four inches before settling back to the terrain while the escape rocket shot free, opened its parachutes, and zig-zagged in the air before falling into the ocean.[9] When President Kennedy, in September 1962, challenged the agency to meet the ambitious goal of landing astronauts on the moon and returning them safely to Earth before the end of the decade, the leaders at NASA realized they had to radically change how they managed projects if they were to have any hope of meeting this ambitious goal.

Instead of working in separate silos and hoping the different parts would somehow come together, NASA's leaders designed a new management approach built upon the principles of "systems think-ing." Contrary to the reductionism of Taylor's scientific management, systems thinking asserts that individual groups cannot effectively accomplish their parts of the work without understanding how the various parts interact to make the whole work.[10] In other words, NASA had to transform its operating management model from a hierarchy to a network. They did this by designing their team and cross-team interactions around the principle of having everybody in the room who was needed to make sound decisions.

The way McChrystal applied this principle was to implement a daily video teleconference, bringing together people from more than seventy locations.[11] These daily sessions included people from all ranks and aspects of the mission. This provided a unique opportunity for a free flow of information among all involved to use the power of their network to create a comprehensive shared understanding of the best way to defeat the enemy's network.

By discarding a rigid command-and-control structure and transforming his organization into a highly adaptable decentralized network, McChrystal was able to easily prevail over the enemy. In making this transformation, McChrystal learned a valuable lesson that applies to many business organizations: Centralized control is ineffec-tive for managing the increasing complexities of twenty-first-century operating environments. While centralized control structures may have worked well for the complicated mechanical environments typ-ical of the twentieth century, hierarchies are ill-equipped to handle the complexities of a hyper-connected, rapidly changing world. In markets where speed and adaptability define success, it takes a net-work to sustain a competitive edge.

THE LEADER'S NEW ROLE

The first step in transitioning from a top-down hierarchy to a peer-to-peer network is to transform the role of the leaders. In peer-to-peer networks, as McChrystal notes, leaders are gardeners, not chess masters. In other words, they are facilitators, not bosses.

Given today's accelerated pace of change, heroic bosses attempting to centrally direct the work of large numbers of people are no match for self-organizing teams who can work faster, smarter, and less expensively thanks to the new tools of mass collaboration. If companies want to succeed in the new economy, they will need to abandon the long-accepted notion that a single intelligent and talented individual can lead organizations to greatness, and they will have to divest managers of their traditional authority to issue orders and expect compliance.

Today, the central challenge of organizing large numbers of workers is about effectively building and leading networks. This means that collective learning and self-organized work replace central planning and hierarchical organization as the foundation for effective strategy and execution. But more importantly, it means that the role of the business leader is no longer to act as a boss. Facilitative leaders don't fit the mold of Lee Iacocca or Jack Welch, the celebrated former CEO at GE. They behave more like the late Bill Gore, the legendary yet humble founder of the company that invented Gore-Tex, or Linus Torvalds, the innovative, unassuming catalyst behind Linux. Digital Age leaders are facilitators responsible for managing the architecture for mass collaboration by creating collective learning processes, building quick consensus, cultivating shared understanding, and keeping companies focused on the few drivers that guide self-managing teams of workers to consistently deliver customer value in fast-changing markets. In the new social technology, the true measure of a leader has more to do with mobilizing human capacity than with motivating individuals.

When the market requires leaders to be facilitators, organizations must be diligent in removing executive ego from the practice of management. Leaders need to understand that building a smart organization is more about leveraging the intelligence of smart teams than amplifying the knowledge of smart individuals. They can only do this if they embrace the humility of the fundamental operating principle of networks that nobody is smarter than everybody. The best way to extinguish the harmful effects of executive ego is to appreciate that leadership is a team responsibility.

In most traditional organizations, the first place to start the transformation from a hierarchy to a network is with the senior leadership team because this is often the most dysfunctional team in the company. What's most troubling is that dysfunction at the top tends to cascade throughout the organization. This was the challenge Alan Mulally faced when he left Boeing to cross industries and become the CEO of the Ford Motor Company.

Transforming the Leadership Team

In the summer of 2006, Bill Ford, the great-grandson of Henry Ford and then CEO of the Ford Motor Company, informed his Board of Directors that the carmaker was in serious trouble. Despite his best efforts, he knew it was time for him to step aside. In a moving speech, Ford humbly and courageously advised his fellow directors that he was not the person who could save the company and asked for their support in helping him find a new CEO for their troubled business.

That's when America's oldest car company turned to Alan Mulally, who, as the leader of the Boeing Company's Airplanes Group, had managed to navigate turbulent waters in the wake of the devastating consequences of September 11, 2001, by transforming the business division into a model of corporate collaboration. While many observers questioned the wisdom of hiring someone outside the automotive industry at such a critical time, Bill Ford knew what he needed most in the next leader of the company that bore his name was not automotive expertise but management savvy.

Before accepting the job, Mulally had been told by members of Ford's board that he should feel free to eliminate any senior executives he felt had to go. However, Mulally replied that he didn't think that would be necessary because he planned to install a team-based management system he called "Working Together" to drive a high level of mutual accountability among the executives.[12]

When he arrived in Dearborn, Mulally found an organization that was fractured, dysfunctional, and more focused on turf battles and political infighting than delighting customers and winning in the marketplace. Nevertheless, he was confident his management system would improve Ford's performance just as it had at Boeing.

The centerpiece of Mulally's system was a two-part weekly session that was mandatory for all senior leaders. The first part of the session was the Business Plan Review, or BPR for short. In the BPR, each senior leadership team member gave a summary of what had happened in the previous week and what was planned for the upcoming week to move key initiatives forward. During the summaries, there was no debate or discussion, which meant there were no opportunities for the one-upmanship or backbiting so typical in the usual corporate meeting. If items needed further discussion, they were handled in the second part of the session, the Special Attention Review, or SAR.

The purpose of the BPR was to stay focused on the big picture and create a transparent environment where people listen for understanding rather than for verbal combat and, most importantly, where individuals could feel safe. This sense of safety in the BPR flowed over to the SAR, where the discussion focused on how team members could help each other solve issues rather than fighting about who was to blame. Like the leaders at NASA, Mulally enabled a dramatic performance turnaround by implementing a management system that gathered everyone needed to make smart decisions in the same room.

Mulally's Working Together system dramatically broke down silos and served as the foundation for a team-based culture that allowed all team members to understand how their parts connected to the whole as departments throughout Ford emulated the BPR/SAR meeting process. As things improved, much like Collins' Level 5 leaders, Mulally looked out the window and credited the team-based management system and the team members for Ford's remarkable turnaround.

The resilience of the Ford Motor Company was a testament to the humility and courage of a great leader who knew when it was time to step aside, another great leader who knew what to do to save a dying company, and the innovative management system that restored Ford to profitability. In 2012, Ford posted a handsome profit of $8 billion.

Cultivating the Leadership Team

General McChrystal and Alan Mulally both understood that a highly effective leadership team is not a collection of heroes where individuals are myopically focused on doing their parts. Both leaders were committed to the notion that leadership is a team responsibility. They knew that teams don't succeed unless members work together to support each other in accomplishing the organization's mission. They recognized that highly effective teams need to be cultivated to achieve the level of collaboration necessary to accomplish extraordinary results. Most importantly, they fully appreciated that cultivating highly effective teams means spending frequent, high-quality time together. For McChrystal, the vehicle was the daily video conference. For Mulally, it was the weekly BPR/SAR meeting. I personally learned the importance of high-quality leadership time when I became a member of the senior leadership team of the Blue Cross Blue Shield Federal Employee Program (FEP).

In the mid-1990s, FEP underwent a major reorganization under the recently appointed chief executive, Steve Gammarino. As part of this restructuring, Steve had replaced all but one of the senior leadership team members. Because so many of us were new to the team, Steve scheduled special weekly all-day meetings for the new leadership group. These were in addition to weekly one-hour staff meetings where the team discussed routine operating issues. The special all-day meetings were held offsite so we could focus on a shared understanding of FEP's strategy and not be distracted by what the people at FranklinCovey refer to as "the whirlwind," which they define as "the massive amount of energy that's necessary just to keep your operation going on a day-to-day basis."[13]

The original intent of these all-day sessions was to lay a solid foundation for working together by assuring we had a firm grasp of our strategic objectives, a solid understanding of how our distributed activities were interconnected, and the necessary tools for supporting each other. We had outlined a comprehensive agenda for accomplishing this work and committed to these weekly meetings until our work was done. The offsite venue provided an environment where we could thoroughly discuss the various items on our agenda without distraction. We took the time needed to address everyone's observations and concerns and develop a shared understanding of key strategic goals. These sessions ensured we all understood the integrated whole of our work together as well as our individual contributions.

These weekly offsite meetings were highly successful. After several weeks, we completed our agenda and built a highly cohesive team. With the agenda complete, we decided to discontinue the offsite sessions and rely on our weekly one-hour staff meetings to coordinate our work going forward. However, a few weeks later, at a staff meeting, one of our team members commented that, while she thought she would be happy to have the time back that was taken up by the all-day offsite meetings, she found she missed the quality of the discussions we had in the sessions and the value they provided for more efficient work. She realized the investment of time in the offsite meetings more than paid itself back because a shared understanding about what we were doing meant things were accomplished in less time, with less cost and higher quality. Others chimed in that they were feeling the same. As one person put it, "While we can't afford the time to have these meetings, what we can't afford even more is not devoting the time to have these sessions."

We all agreed we needed to reestablish the offsite, all-day meeting discipline. Only this time, we felt meeting bi-weekly would be best because the work of solid team building had been accomplished. Going forward, what we needed was the quality time that would allow us to continue the cultivation of our team. We had learned, in the words of General McChrystal, that a gardener's work is never done.

In 2001, I succeeded Steve as FEP's chief executive when he assumed a larger role within the Blue Cross Blue Shield organization. Unlike many new leaders, I didn't need to fix a broken system.

I inherited a highly capable and extraordinary leadership team. My job was to continue cultivating this incredible group's combined talents. And the best way to do that was to maintain the gardening that occurred in our bi-weekly, offsite meetings.

Focusing on What's Most Important

Because it seems completely counterintuitive, the practice of bi-weekly, all-day meetings is one of the most difficult habits for business leaders to adopt. With so many urgent problems and crises bombarding the business, most leaders feel there simply isn't time to engage in all-day group dialogues. While they would like to devote more time to thinking about the business and would certainly do so if they felt they had a choice, as a practical matter, most senior executives feel they have more important things that must be done. Leaders in this frame of mind confuse what's most urgent with what's most important and are likely caught up in the whirlwind.

Because operations are the primary source of a business's most pressing problems, the more urgent the issues, the greater the intensity of the whirlwind. A highly intense whirlwind is the enemy of innovation. It makes it hard to execute anything new and robs business leaders of the focus needed to move the business forward.[14] This describes what happened to Blockbuster when it passed on the opportunity to acquire Netflix and build a new business model. Instead, the video king eventually went bankrupt because it lacked the discipline to focus on what's most important. Although it may seem counterintuitive, when senior leadership teams devote high-quality time to what's most important, they are far better able to adapt to fast-changing markets. This was our experience at FEP.

Our bi-weekly offsite sessions began by setting the agenda for the day. While a tentative list of topics was usually distributed a day or two before the session, the meeting's final agenda was always established in the first twenty minutes. Our first order of business was to confirm our continuing strategic priorities. We followed a discipline to maintain no more than four top priorities to ensure we had a clear sense of focus. Having too many priorities runs the risk that few, if any, will be accomplished and certainly none with excellence. Our top priorities were typically the first four items on our tentative agenda. Most times, the priorities were confirmed. However, occasionally a team member might propose a new priority for the group's consideration. If we decided to add the topic, it meant we needed to remove another item from the list. Our commitment to designate only four strategic issues was the most difficult and important part of our team discipline because we forced ourselves to make the hard choices necessary to be a highly focused organization.

As team members continued to propose potential agenda for the day, the team's leader recorded the items on a flip chart, including the topic's sponsor and the estimated time needed to thoroughly discuss each item. When the list was complete, the group would quickly designate topics as "A" or "B" items by consensus. A items needed to be discussed that day; B items could wait for the next session, if necessary. Each of the A items was then assigned a specific time slot. Any remaining time was assigned to selected items from the B list.

The team leader's primary role in these all-day meetings was to manage our time to make sure that all A items were understood thoroughly and handled sufficiently. The content of each topic was facilitated by the sponsor who proposed or was primarily responsible for the issue. This practice ensured that leadership for the content of our discussions was distributed across the team. In addition to managing time, another important role for the team's leader was to recognize when the group was stuck and shift the dynamic of the discussion to help move the group along. For example, the leader might split the team into two groups and ask them to focus on innovative ways to meet apparently contradictory needs. Another way the leader might move the group along is to ask to hear from one person at a time, with no questions, comments, or interruptions until everyone has a chance to speak. Shifting the dynamics of the discussion usually deepened the team's understanding, allowing us to move forward to a workable consensus.

This highly valuable practice makes sure that leadership teams have a thorough and shared understanding of the most important strategic issues affecting the business. By deeply understanding what's most important, leadership teams are far more likely to make better decisions. We can only wonder if Blockbuster had adopted this practice, perhaps they might have bought Netflix when they had that golden opportunity.

A New Leadership Paradigm

There is no place for heroic leaders in Digital Age businesses. In a rapidly changing, hyper-connected world, the locus of leadership is the team, and the most important work of the leadership team is making sure the organizational infrastructure supports the collective learning and shared understanding that workers need to self-manage their efforts. In peer-to-peer network enterprises, there are no bosses or subordinates; there are only workers. The collective team of leaders, not the singular boss, is the star.

This team-based approach to leadership is a paradigm shift that diminishes, if not eliminates, the traditional supervisor-subordinate relationship. This paradigm shift can be hard to fully grasp, even for companies who have had the good fortune to hire a chief executive who practices team-based self-management. Far too often, when these great leaders move on, the peer-to-peer infrastructure they cultivated reverts to a top-down hierarchy, especially when the successor is a classic heroic leader.

For example, when Mark Fields replaced Alan Mulally as Ford's CEO in the summer of 2014, the business author Bryce Hoffman recounts in a 2017 *Forbes* article that many reporters asked him at the time how he thought Fields would fare. Hoffman told them, "Alan has given Mark the skills he needs to run Ford and left him with a management system and strategic vision that can ensure the company's future success."[15] But Hoffman also provided an important caveat, "It's going to take a big man to sit on his hands and not try to fix what isn't broken."[16] Great leaders understand this. Unfortunately, heroic

76

leaders frequently do not because a misplaced, perhaps distorted, sense of responsibility compels them to believe their success will only be recognized if they make an individual difference. Often, this is an unconscious sense that plays out by retooling the management system to make it clear that there is a new leader. If this retooling improves upon previous practices, success will likely be sustained. However, if the prime purpose of the retooling is to convey there's a new person in charge, this can lead to a significant reduction in performance. Unfortunately, as Hoffman quotes one of his sources, "Mark had to make it his own."[17] Ford's performance deteriorated, and Fields was let go in 2017.

Management System or Management Style

It's interesting to note that, according to Hoffman, when Mulally left Boeing in 2006 and Ford in 2014, his successors dismantled his Working Together management system, allowing bureaucracy to creep back in.[18] For all practical purposes, what Mulally considered a management system was perceived by his superiors and his successors as his idiosyncratic management style. This can be a problem for sustaining extraordinary performance. Often, when leaders who have behaved as gardeners move on, several forces come into play to reinforce the old chess master role. Board members unaware of the importance of choosing what Collins calls Level 5 leaders are prone to view the former leader's gardening approach as a style preference rather than a difference maker. Thus, they are susceptible to hiring heroic leaders who typically lack the skills to lead a powerful peer-to-peer network. The new leaders themselves are often an obstacle because they are likely more comfortable and experienced with the chess master role. Finally, any peer executives to the former leader who felt threatened by or disagreed with the peer-to-peer management approach are likely to behave like antibodies in an immune system, highly motivated to restore traditional management practices by squashing the new ways of working. This is especially true when gardeners who moved on have led business units inside a larger organization.

Mulally and McChrystal were Level 5 leaders who each built great organizations that were extraordinarily successful. Neither leader attributed their success to personal acumen but to a system based on the notion that greatness is more about smart teams than heroic leaders. However, the system that each of these leaders installed was not baked into the essential DNA of the organization. McChrystal had the wherewithal to build a peer-to-peer network structure inside a larger hierarchical organization that continues to be a top-down enterprise. Mulally temporarily transformed both the airplane unit he led at Boeing and the Ford Motor Company. However, when he left each of these organizations, the overarching structure was still a top-down hierarchy. The supervisor-subordinate relationship had never been dismantled. As long as companies have bosses, these organizations are prone to devolve into top-down bureaucracies.

Unless leaders who behave as gardeners completely dismantle the underlying hierarchical structure by eliminating the traditional supervisor-subordinate relationship and replacing it with peer-to-peer team-based decision-making, the network dynamics they put in place are unlikely to extend beyond their tenure. In that case, the network model that leaders practice is not the installation of a management system but is, in fact, the exercise of a management style. The true transformation of an organization into a peer-to-peer team-based network is only possible if successor leaders do not have the ability to use singular command authority to reinstate the hierarchical structure. When this is so, the peer-to-peer team-based network has succeeded in remolding the inherent DNA of the organization.

There is good news and bad news for those who work inside traditional organizations and want to leverage collective intelligence and the synergistic power of networks to lead extraordinary performance. The good news is that it is possible for leaders to build effective networked teams inside bureaucratic organizations if they think very differently. They will need to appreciate that leadership is more about intellectual honesty than intellectual prowess, emotional intelligence than academic smarts, personal humility than self-promoting confidence, a strong will than a strong ego, and building shared understanding than taking charge. If leaders can transform their thinking and learn to be gardeners, they can build very powerful teams inside their organizations.

The bad news is that unless gardener-style leaders have the authority to dismantle all vestiges of the hierarchical structure completely and permanently, the organizations left behind will likely revert to traditional management practices when they move on. Despite all their rhetoric about being part of a team and working together, most traditional leaders don't appreciate that great leadership is a team effort. They still believe in management superheroes and think it's all about them.

But what if you don't want your organization to revert to a hierarchy when you move on? Or what if you are an entrepreneur and the leader of a wildly successful and rapidly growing company that you don't ever want to become a bureaucracy? What would it take to bake the team-based peer-to-peer network into the DNA of your company so that it's incredibly difficult, if not impossible, to ever devolve into a top-down hierarchy? Suppose you have the management courage to become a facilitative leader and forgo the temptation to take charge and control everything around you. In that case, building a permanent peer-to-peer network organization where team-based decision-making catalyzes extraordinary performance is possible. In the next chapter, we will visit three very successful companies with no bosses or assignments because no one in the company has command authority.

5

SELF-MANAGEMENT PIONEERS

According to Frederic Laloux, the author of *Reinventing Organizations: A Guide for Creating Organizations Inspired by the
Next Stage of Human Consciousness*, the days of the top-down
hierarchy as the dominant organizational framework may be num-
bered. Despite its continued preference by the current power elite,
the bureaucratic management model is rapidly becoming limited and
obsolete now that the technology revolution has unleashed the extraordinary and unstoppable phenomenon of distributed intelligence.[1]

Laloux points out that organizations are expressions of the dominant worldviews of their times. His extensive research traces the
evolution of organizations over the past 10,000 years. Over that
period, Laloux noticed whenever we change the fundamental way
we think about the world, we come up with new and more powerful
types of organizations, and while prior forms of organizations don't
completely disappear, the higher-order organizational frameworks
that evolve from new ways of thinking tend to become the dominant
practice of the new age. Laloux also noticed that these passages from
one age to another are not continuous, gradual transitions but sudden
transformations, and most importantly, he suggests that we are in
the midst of one of these transformations right now.[2]

Using a color-coded typology inspired by the work of Clare Graves
and made popular by Don Beck and Christopher Cowan in their
book *Spiral Dynamics*, Laloux outlines the evolution of four types
of organizations over the last ten millennia and describes in detail

the attributes and characteristics of a fifth and radically different emerging organizational form.

The first of the four historical types is the *Red* organization, which appeared about 10,000 years ago when people were organized into chiefdoms. The fundamental rubric in these small groups is the exercise of overwhelming personal power through fear or submission to keep organizations intact. This type of organization is highly reactive and focused on the short term. Current examples of Red organizations include the Mafia, street gangs, and tribal militias.[3]

The second type is the *Amber* organization. Organizational life dramatically shifted when the agricultural revolution transformed nomadic hunter-gatherers into settled farmers and gave rise to the first bureaucracies with the emergence of political states, social institutions, and organized religions. In Amber organizations, authority is linked to formal roles rather than to powerful personalities. These roles are arrayed in strict chains of command to direct all aspects of social activity. One of the great breakthroughs of bureaucracy is its capacity for long-term planning and scalability, which enables the accomplishment of complicated endeavors. Current examples, according to Laloux, include the Catholic Church, the military, and most government agencies.[4]

The Industrial Revolution generated the next type, the *Orange* organization. While Orange organizations retain the hierarchical pyramid as their basic structure, followers are given more autonomy in how to accomplish management directives. Nevertheless, consistent with the industrial worldview, organizations are viewed as machines that need to be manipulated and controlled by their leaders. Thus, these organizations can feel lifeless and soulless despite the small freedom workers have in performing their tasks. The multinational company is a current example of an Orange organization.[5]

The fourth historical type is the *Green* organization. This next iteration is a response to the shadow side of the Orange organization. With the increased educational level of workers, especially in the second half of the twentieth century, organizational leaders became uneasy with the exercise of hierarchical power. Thus, Green organizations emphasize the importance of empowerment, striving for bottom-up processes, gathering input from all, and building consensus. However, despite their focus on creating strong human cultures, Green organizations are still hierarchies because the notion of empowerment is predicated on the premise that the leaders have the authority to choose whether to delegate their power. As long as the leaders choose to delegate, they remain Green. However, if a new leader comes along who doesn't care about culture, these organizations can quickly morph back to Orange. This is what happened at both Boeing and Ford when Alan Mulally left each of the two companies. Laloux cites Southwest Airlines, Ben & Jerry's, and DaVita as current examples of Green companies.[6]

THE TEAL ORGANIZATION

The one common feature of the four historical models is bosses. From the first chiefs to present-day CEOs, the exercise of power has been about "being in charge." Even in the empowerment structures of Green organizations, the people in charge have to delegate their power for empowerment to take hold. But Laloux asks, "What if we could create organizational structures that didn't need empowerment because, by design, everybody was powerful, and no one was powerless?"[7] In other words, what if we could create organizations where power wasn't a function of being in charge, and thus, there were no bosses? The answer, according to Laloux, is the *Teal* organization.

The Teal organization is a revolutionary new management model that operates from the premise that organizations should be viewed as living organisms and, therefore, function more like complex adaptive systems than machines. Accordingly, this organizational form is a flexible and fluid peer relationship structure where work is accomplished through self-managed teams.

Teal organizations have no layers of middle management, very few staff, and very few rules or control mechanisms. Instead of reporting to single supervisors, people are accountable to the members of their teams for accomplishing self-organized, collective goals. As counterintuitive as it may seem, eliminating controlling bosses typically enables a better-controlled organization because peer pressure is a more effective performance motivator than compliance. In describing the dynamics of Teal organizations, Laloux points out, "The heart of the matter is that workers and employees are seen as reasonable people who can be trusted to do the right thing."[8] In other words, a distinguishing characteristic separating self-managed, peer-to-peer networks from centralized, top-down hierarchies is that the facilitators of networks trust people a lot more than the take-charge bosses in hierarchies.

While there are no bosses in Teal organizations, these are not leaderless enterprises. In fact, Teal organizations have more leaders than their hierarchical counterparts because they can tap into the leadership capabilities of everyone within the organization. In Teal organizations, all voices count because anyone can sense a problem or opportunity. Additionally, since anyone can be a leader, everyone has the wherewithal to recruit followers to determine whether they need to do something. If enough people join, action is taken; nothing is done if recruits can't be found. What makes these peer-to-peer networks so efficient, in comparison to top-down hierarchies, is their inherent ability to leverage their collective intelligence as a powerful resource for responding to fast-changing circumstances.

In a relatively stable world where all social institutions share the same hierarchical paradigm, leveraging the individual intelligence of the few is a workable premise for designing organizations. For over 10,000 years, there was no practical competition for the top-down hierarchical paradigm and no incentive to change for those who enjoyed the lucrative benefits of being on the top of these pyramids. However, this is changing because, as advances in digital technology continue to pressure organizations to be faster and more adaptable, business leaders will eventually—and perhaps suddenly—discover that the only way they can respond to this pressure is to transform themselves into Teal organizations. While this may rightly appear to be a daunting task, let's visit three companies that have successfully used the peer-to-peer network organizational model to sustain business success over multiple decades.

A Lattice Organization

There are no bosses at W.L. Gore and Associates, and there have never been since the company was founded in 1958. For over sixty years, the makers of Gore-Tex and countless other innovative products have used shared understanding and self-management to build a very successful learning organization with over $3.8 billion in annual revenue and more than 11,000 associates in thirty countries worldwide. With its enviable track record of innovation and sustained profitability, Gore is living proof that corporations can organize large numbers of people into a sustainable business without bosses.

While Gore has a CEO and a small number of designated leaders for its major divisions and its companywide support functions, such as human resources and information technology, these leaders don't assign work to anyone.[9] Nobody at Gore—not even the CEO—tells anyone what to do or how to do it. There are no vice presidents or supervisors; there are only associates. Some of the associates may serve as leaders from time to time, but another leader never assigns this role. If you want to lead a project at Gore, you have to recruit followers. In true self-organizing form, the followers determine the leaders, and the leaders remain in their roles as long as they maintain their peers' respect and support. This eliminates a systemic flaw that often plagues traditional organizations by ensuring leaders can't abuse positional power because they have none.[10]

For the most part, leadership at Gore is not a permanently assigned position but a temporary role that is continually earned for as long as a particular project may last. Even when selecting who will fill those few designated leadership positions, the associates usually have a voice in the choice. Terri Kelly, who served as Gore's CEO from 2005 until her retirement in 2018, describes how she was selected to be Gore's key leader. Kelly explains that, upon the retirement of her predecessor, the board of directors polled a wide cross-section of Gore associates and asked them whom they'd be willing to follow. "We weren't given a list of names—we were free to choose anyone in the company," Kelly recalls. "To my surprise, it was me."[11]

When Bill Gore started his company in 1958, he had just concluded a seventeen-year stint with DuPont. He was familiar with the workings of traditional companies and knew that he wanted his new business venture to be different, especially in how people communicated with each other. Gore often said that, in hierarchical organizations, "communication really happens in the carpool," meaning that the ride to and from work was the only place where people felt free to talk to each other without worrying about the chain of command.[12] Gore did not want any conversation impediments in his new company because he understood the free interchange of ideas was the soil of innovation. Gore was clearly ahead of his time in recognizing that conversation would become the catalyst that would drive the corporation. Therefore, Gore built what he called a lattice organization where there would be no traditional organization charts, chain of command, or predetermined communication channels. Unlike the top-down hierarchy, a lattice-based architecture connects everyone in the organization to everyone else to form a dense network of peer-to-peer connections where information flows in all directions, unfiltered by intermediaries.[13]

Bill Gore's organizational approach was extraordinarily innovative for the 1950s. In his lattice organization, all work is self-managed by teams, and projects are accepted rather than assigned. Workers are partners and volunteers accountable to their teams rather than a boss. Everyone is free to talk to anyone else in the organization, and people are expected to be open and candid when Gore associates gather for meetings. Compensation is determined using a peer review process, similar to law firms. On average, every associate evaluates twenty people and is evaluated by twenty peers. Thus, the associates are rewarded based on their contributions to team success and are incentivized to commit to more rather than less work.[14]

There is no central planning at Gore and Associates. No single person or elite group determines strategy, sets the direction, or drives execution. The collective intelligence of the associates determines strategy, and because there are no bosses, no one individual can kill a good idea or keep a worthless project alive. All voices count at Gore, and how many associates are willing to work on the proposition determines whether a project goes forward. Once a project goes forward, the self-managed team determines its direction and requirements based on the team's shared understanding.

Gore's consistent success for well over six decades is clear proof that the decentralized collective wisdom of workers is an alternative to the centralized planning of a managerial elite. However, as the digital revolution continues to radically transform the world, we will likely find that companies such as Gore are better capable of managing at the new pace of change and responding to the market's increasing demands for knowledge and speed. While on the surface Gore's approach to strategy and execution may seem haphazard and inefficient, their outstanding performance in developing innovative products across various industries is a testament to the reality that nobody is smarter or faster than everybody.

It is perhaps ironic that an engineer trained in mechanical thinking was the one who built the first large corporation designed as a self-managed, peer-to-peer network. While he knew from his previous experiences at DuPont that bosses could drive results, Gore was convinced that the workers would achieve better results if his organization had the processes to hear and aggregate all their perspectives. Without any bosses, no one could silence a voice or abuse the power of position to coerce a mandated point of view. By tying compensation to performance and using a collective peer review process to determine everyone's pay, Gore assured the associates would be working for and listening to each other and have an incentive to collaborate to produce the best results for the company. Gore understood that peer pressure is a far more effective motivator than pleasing the boss as long as you have the right social infrastructure.

Early on, Bill Gore learned two prerequisites were critical to using the collective intelligence of his workers to drive strategy and execution. First, all the different contributors needed to be together in the same place. This means that product design, sales, marketing, and production staff work together in cross-functional teams. Hence, everyone continually understands how their contributions shape and reshape the underlying business processes of the company's value proposition. Gore recognized the importance of having teams focused on collective processes rather than individual tasks to enable performance excellence.

Second, Bill Gore noticed that things got awkward when the number of workers reached about 150 to 200 people. There seems to be a tipping point in the human scale where the effectiveness of peer pressure and physical ability to self-organize begins to break down.[15] When more than 200 people are in the same location, the individuals don't feel as personally connected, and it becomes difficult to know everyone's name. We can understand why, in the early factories of the Industrial Age, the owners resorted to hierarchical management to organize the work of large numbers of people. When the efforts of a sizable group of workers have to be brought together, and there are so many they can't possibly all know each other, the corporate pioneers of mass production felt that authoritative bosses were necessary to get the job done. Bill Gore, however, did not want to resort to the employment of bosses when he noticed the tipping point. Instead, he implemented a simple practice to preserve his self-organizing management innovation that continues today. When a plant approaches two hundred people, the group divides, and Gore opens another plant. The new plant may be a stone's throw from the original location, but each plant is completely autonomous to ensure the human scale necessary for self-management to work.

What Bill Gore learned intuitively from his experience in growing his lattice organization was confirmed empirically by the renowned British anthropologist Robin Dunbar. In 1993, Dunbar published a paper that presented the results of his examination of the relationship between brain size and group size in cohesive groups of primates. Dunbar noticed when human groups exceed 150 people, individuals are less likely to work effectively together or lend a helping hand.[16] This number has come to be known as Dunbar's number and is a critical factor in building self-managed, peer-to-peer networks. It determines the maximum group size in which everyone can recognize each other and maintain stable, coherent relationships, which

Dunbar defines as "one that can be picked up again on meeting after an absence without any need to reestablish where you stand."[17]

As Bill Gore discovered, a foundation of stable, familiar relationships is essential for maintaining a high-performing, self-managed network. It also enables an environment that fosters innovation because small, cross-functional, autonomous units are more capable of adapting to changing circumstances or emergent opportunities. The management author Gary Hamel points out that self-managed organizations may have a competitive advantage because "most executives overweight the advantages of scale and underweight the advantage of flexibility."[18] If adaptability is to be an organizational core competency, the size of the autonomous working group should not exceed 150 people.

Bill Gore was very proud of his lattice organization's egalitarian principles and practices. Gore wanted all associates to know that he considered them partners on a shared journey toward innovative excellence. Even though Gore and Associates is a privately held company, after their first year at Gore, new associates receive 12 percent of their salary in company stock, which the partners can cash out if they leave after they are fully vested.[19] The stock's appreciation depends on the company's ability to continue growing, and independent consultants periodically determine its value.[20] At Gore and Associates, every worker is treated as a partner with a stake in the company's profits.

Perhaps Bill Gore's greatest accomplishment is that his vision of a lattice organization without bosses lives on long after he died in 1986. Gore and Associates demonstrate that companies built around shared understanding and self-organization are not subject to disruptions when successful leaders move on. Succession planning and consistent execution are not issues when companies are guided by the collective wisdom and shared understanding of the workers and when organizations truly appreciate that workers are partners, not subordinates.

Two Core Principles

Chris Rufer was another leader who wanted his business organization to be very different. In 1970, Rufer, a recent MBA graduate, founded Morning Star, which was originally a one-person trucking operation hauling tomatoes.[21] As he became more familiar with the tomato processing industry, Rufer began recognizing ways to make the work more efficient. Unable to convince industry insiders to adopt his ideas, Rufer assembled a group of investors and opened his first processing plant in 1983. However, within a few years, he and his investors had unreconcilable differences about the company's direction and organizational philosophy. Eventually, Rufer sold his interest in the processing plant.[22]

In 1990, free of his investors and the sole owner of his company, Rufer opened a new facility near Los Banos, California. In designing how the organization in his new plant should work, Rufer chose to think differently and design a company where there would be no bosses, and work would be self-organized by the employees. At the time, the idea that you could build a successful enterprise without bosses would have been considered business insanity. The notion that employees could effectively self-organize work defied all conventional wisdom on how to build a successful enterprise. But Chris Rufer is not a conventional businessman. According to Doug Kirkpatrick, who served as financial controller on the new facility's startup team, Rufer asked the group to structure the company based on two core ideas: No one has the authority to use force against another person, and everyone should keep their commitments to each other and to the company mission.

Guided by these two core principles, the startup team crafted an organization without supervisors. Instead, all colleagues, as Morning Star refers to its employees, would work for the company mission. In other words, as Kirkpatrick points out, "The mission is the boss." Accordingly, each colleague prepares a personal mission statement describing how he or she will contribute to the company's mission of "producing tomato products and services which consistently achieve the quality and service expectations of our customers."[23]

In terms of day-to-day structure, from the beginning, Morning Star has been a collection of relatively autonomous business teams. Each team has a clear mission that serves as the context for the mission statements of the individual colleagues.[24] The teams are responsible for determining their decision rights as they see fit for various circumstances. For example, a team could delegate the call to a single expert if a decision requires specific technical know-how. In other situations, the team may agree upon a majority vote, unanimous vote, or designated subgroup consensus to make the decision.

While many business leaders might have been skeptical of what Rufer called self-management, the two core principles of noncoercion and commitment to the mission laid the foundation for a successful business enterprise. Rufer demonstrated a simple alternative management model that can sustain extraordinary results. Together with a peer process to mediate disagreements between colleagues—each of whom has an equal voice in the organization—these two principles essentially represented the entire enterprise governance for the first six years until 1996, when Morning Star built its second factory and effectively doubled its size.

The coordination needed to scale a fast-growing business while maintaining Morning Star's core principles led to the creation of a new instrument designed to support a peer-to-peer network where individual colleagues negotiate specific commitments with each other and continuously measure and monitor the status of these agreements. Morning Star named this instrument the Colleague Letter of Understanding (CLOU).

At least annually, colleagues in the various business units gather to discuss business strategy, negotiating or updating their CLOUs with co-workers directly affected. Typically, a colleague negotiates with about seven to twelve other colleagues. A completed CLOU lists several specific deliverables with relevant performance metrics. The negotiation and documented agreement of measurable deliverables form the basis of the shared understanding that directs the coordination of the individual efforts of each contributor. By holding colleagues accountable to each other rather than supervisors, Morning Star creates a highly collaborative environment where everyone effectively becomes each other's customer.

Throughout the year, detailed business information is updated and made available to all colleagues to track the metrics in their own and their co-workers' CLOUs. The transparency of critical financial and operational data is essential for self-management to work well. Unless people have real-time access to data throughout the year, negotiating CLOUs runs the risk of becoming nothing more than an empty exercise. When coupled with these data-driven metrics, called Steppingstones because they are considered steppingstones to superior performance, CLOUs can be a lever that drives extraordinary business results.

In designing Morning Star's organizational system, Rufer and his colleagues preferred the structural values of collective intelligence, iterative discovery, synergistic power, diversity of opinion, and agreement. In so doing, they embodied the essential design principle of peer-to-peer networks: Nobody is smarter than everybody.

Accordingly, Morning Star's organizational model leverages the collective intelligence of all colleagues by giving them the ability to be fully involved and make their own decisions through a negotiation process that respects diversity of opinion and honors all voices without censorship or fear of retaliation. No one has the coercive power to silence or dominate another person.

There is no such thing as insubordination in a peer-to-peer network because the goal of this innovative management model is not compliance but agreement freely made by every contributor. What is fascinating about Morning Star's social structure is how it completely revolutionizes how power works by shifting the basis of power from coercion to synergy. This shift is game-changing because it allows the building of a healthier, more intelligent, and more powerful human system than its hierarchical counterparts.

It turns out you can get a lot done when no one is in charge, as Gary Hamel, the celebrated management consultant, discovered when he visited Morning Star. After touring its main facility and becoming familiar with Morning Star's unconventional organizational practices, Hamel commented to Rufer that the innovative company had discovered how to manage without managers. Rufer saw it differently and pointed out that at Morning Star, everyone is a manager because everyone is responsible for the resources needed to get the job done and for holding colleagues accountable for accomplishing the company's mission.[25]

Today, the company where everyone is a manager has grown into the world's largest tomato processor, with nearly $1 billion in annual revenue, around 500 full-time colleagues, and more than 2,000 seasonal colleagues during the summer harvest season.

Humanity Over Bureaucracy

Another organization that leverages synergistic power is Buurtzorg, which provides home health services in the Netherlands. Buurtzorg was founded in 2006 by Jos de Blok, a nurse who had a radical idea for a better way to organize neighborhood nurses—an idea he knew would never be accepted in the traditional organization where he worked.

In the Dutch healthcare system, neighborhood nurses are essential, working hand-in-hand with hospitals and family doctors.[26] At the time, every one of the approximately eighty-five nursing organizations followed the traditional bureaucratic model where the primary focus was on efficiency and economies of scale. Accordingly, the various tasks of these organizations were distributed into specific functional roles, such as intake specialists, schedule planners, call center employees, and, of course, managers and supervisors.

What concerned de Blok was that, although this typical arrangement was highly efficient, it unwittingly enabled a system that lost track of patients as human beings.[27] For example, because schedule planning was done by people who didn't know the patients and whose primary interest was minimizing the travel time of nurses between visits, the patients had no continuity of care. They would see different nurses from visit to visit. While the system appeared to be managing costs well, the same could not be said for managing patient care.

To correct this problem, de Blok put in place an organizational arrangement where nurses work in self-managed teams of ten to twelve professionals, with each team responsible for the care of fifty patients in well-defined neighborhoods.[28] From day one, no one on the teams has ever been in charge, and there is no prescribed division of labor. Instead, the teams are responsible for collectively distributing tasks among themselves, monitoring their performance and productivity, and making important decisions that affect the team.

Jos de Blok's innovative organizational paradigm has been extraordinarily successful. In its first seven years, Buurtzorg rapidly grew from ten to 7,000 nurses and, today employs two-thirds of all neighborhood nurses in the Netherlands.[29] Buurtzorg requires almost 40 percent fewer hours of care per patient than traditional nursing organizations because, by putting patient care first, Buurtzorg's clients heal faster, are less likely to be hospitalized, and stay in care half as long.[30] It turns out the key to efficiency has less to do with focusing on costs and managing travel time between visits and more to do with providing a human-care experience for the patients.

Today, Buurtzorg employs 15,000 nurses and domestic helpers organized into a network of 1,200 self-managing teams.[31] Each team is responsible for making decisions for finding patients, securing office space, scheduling staff, managing budgets, and recruiting new team members. Everyone on the teams has an equal voice in crafting the mutual agreements that guide the coordinated activities of the team members. Buurtzorg's unconventional self-management model eliminates bureaucracy from its day-to-day operations. In fact, Buurtzorg's motto is "Humanity above bureaucracy."[32]

ORGANIZATIONS DESIGNED TO LEARN

W.L. Gore and Associates, Morning Star, and Buurtzorg are testaments to the practical and extraordinary capabilities of self-managed, peer-to-peer networks. These Teal organizations represent the future of management because they have the single most important core competency for sustained success in a rapidly changing and increasingly complex business environment: *the inherent organizational capacity to learn*. This capacity provides self-managed, peer-to-peer networks with a distinct competitive advantage over traditional companies whose top-down structures foster a proclivity for maintaining the status quo. In a world where the prevalent business mantra is change or die, businesses that can't adapt run the risk of becoming extinct, no matter how successful they may have been in the past.

One of the first business thought leaders to recognize the importance of learning as a critical core competency is Peter Senge, who, in his seminal work, *The Fifth Discipline: The Art and Practice of the Learning Organization*, contends that most companies are short-lived because they suffer from fatal learning disabilities.[33] Senge's contention is particularly relevant to today's dynamic business environment because, in fast-changing times, whether an organization has a competent learning capacity may determine whether a company survives.

Businesses can no longer afford to impose top-down corporate views that distort or are completely out of touch with reality. By the time the errors are realized, it may be too late to act. Accordingly, learning organizations encourage work cultures of reflection and inquiry where anyone can challenge existing assumptions, and workers are expected to drive innovation.

Because no one can command or control another colleague in self-managed, peer-to-peer networks, companies like Gore, Morning Star, and Buurtzorg are natural learning organizations. They recognize that success in demanding, rapidly changing markets calls for colleagues who are intrinsically committed to the company's mission and are focused on learning and collaborating to discover new ways to delight their customers. This is in stark contrast to the command-and-control organization where the vision of an elite few is the mandate of the many, consistently reinforced by an externally directed reward-and-punishment control structure.

The leaders of learning organizations fully appreciate that nobody is smarter than everybody. They understand that genuine team learning requires a different kind of discourse from the limited conversational norms of command-and-control organizations. Specifically, the debate and defensiveness of traditional organizations must be replaced with dialogue and inquiry. Success in the twenty-first-century marketplace belongs to companies skilled at achieving value-added, win-win, synergistic solutions rather than the hollow win-lose political victories so common in hierarchical organizations.

Senge identifies systems thinking as the cornerstone of management practice in the learning organization. Leaders who engage in systems thinking recognize that reactive linear thinking solutions are often no solution but short-term fixes that only postpone and exacerbate root problems. In fast-paced markets where customer needs rapidly evolve in response to technological innovations, companies that rely on short-term, shortsighted quick fixes will lose their place in the market or go out of business altogether. The complex business problems of the twenty-first century require proactive, thoughtful, and, most importantly, holistic solutions based on a firm understanding of how the parts of a business interrelate. Increasingly, crafting holistic solutions calls for aggregating the collective intelligence of autonomous, cross-functional teams. The capacity to leverage collective intelligence is the essential dynamic that defines the learning organization and, as the pioneers of self-management have successfully demonstrated, the modus operandi of the self-managed peer-to-peer network.

6

AN EXTRAORDINARY
LEAP IN INTELLIGENCE

When John Antioco, the CEO of Blockbuster, turned down the offer to buy Netflix in early 2000, which we discussed in Chapter 2, he made the single most foolish decision in Blockbuster's history. Antioco's judgment that the internet was completely overblown and would have no impact on his industry would prove fatally flawed when all but one Blockbuster store rapidly disappeared beginning in 2010. The failure to invest $50 million to develop an online video capability would cost the then $6 billion enterprise the opportunity to grow fifty-fold to over $300 billion— Netflix's market value in 2021.[1] This failure likely happened because centralized, top-down organizations have an Achilles' heel. Hierarchies are overdependent upon solo decision-makers whose judgments are often hampered by two types of blind spots: unknown unknowns and unconscious biases. Unless leaders take steps to become conscious of these blind spots, they and their organizations are likely to fall victim to the hubris that plagues companies that rest on the laurels of past successes, especially when the world is rapidly changing. While the steps that need to be taken are simple, most business leaders will have difficulty freeing themselves from the hazards of blind spots because embracing these steps requires a radical change in how we define the critical work of management.

The Critical Work of Management

The *Oxford English Dictionary* defines management as the process of dealing with or controlling things or people. For the typical hierarchical leader, management equals control. This explains why so many executives are invested in extending their span of control. Whether moving to a higher position in the hierarchy or assuming greater responsibilities by increasing the number of people reporting to them, most traditional executives gauge management advancement by the extent of their span of control. When the core values for designing an organization are elite intelligence, central planning, coercive power, uniformity of thought, and compliance, it makes sense that the central focus that drives organizational effectiveness is control, which explains why we refer to the top-down organization as command-and-control management.

However, is control the essence of management, especially as business problems shift from complicated to complex? For most of the twentieth century, business problems were complicated concerns that were essentially mechanical. Solutions could generally be found by applying linear and reductionist thinking. Accordingly, solving a problem meant finding the part that wasn't working properly, calling an expert to fix it, and reconfiguring the parts to work more effectively. For example, if constructing a key part of the rudder system on an airplane causes the rudder to move opposite the direction intended by the pilot, the problem is solved by reengineering the part to follow the pilot's intended action.

An elemental attribute of machines is that we can take them apart, examine their parts separately, and put them back together in working order. We can also experiment with new parts or rearrange the components to find ways for the machine to work more effectively. This is what mechanics do all the time. It's also what business leaders do when they use Frederick Taylor's management principles to solve problems or move the parts around in corporate reorganizations. This thinking works for managing machines because control is the fundamental dynamic for operating inanimate objects. However, does this thinking work for managing people?

The history of business throughout the twentieth century would seem to support the workability of Taylor's reductionist model because the top-down hierarchy has been the near-universal organizational structure for managing people for all this time. However, this dominance may have more to do with the mechanical nature of the business problems to be solved than with the assumed effectiveness of the model for people management.

What happens when the problems are complex matters rather than complicated concerns? This evolution in business issues changes the underlying context for finding solutions because, rather than being mechanical, complex problems are organic and can't be solved with reductionist thinking, as we recently learned with the creation of an experimental vaccine as a simplistic one-size-fits-all solution to rid the world of a new virus. This solution was doomed to fail because viruses are evolutionary organisms. In their myopic approach to the problem of the pandemic, the elite experts seemed to be blind to the collateral damage they fostered on human development, health maintenance, social cohesion, institutional trust, and financial stability. Unlike the airplane rudder issue, complex problems cannot be solved by linear thinking or control-oriented management systems. They can only be solved by taking a holistic perspective and engaging in systems thinking. If the business of business is solving complex problems, Taylor's reductionist management system will not work for either issue or people management.

When the world is rapidly changing, and problems are becoming increasingly complex, organizations cannot afford to be exposed to the hazards of the blind spots of unconscious biases and unknown unknowns. A focus on control does not protect against these blind spots. In fact, overcontrolling behavior can be completely counterproductive, as we learned in Chapter 2 when Captain McBroom's myopic judgment calls led to the crash of United 173. The crucial work of management is not about the expansion of control; it's about the expansion of consciousness. It's about discovering the unknown unknowns and uncovering unconscious biases.

Consciousness is the critical work of management because it expands personal and organizational competence, improving decision making. Antioco and McBroom failed in their decisions because the combination of control authority and innate blind spots caused normally competent individuals to become highly incompetent in rapidly changing circumstances. This combination also paralyzed organizational effectiveness because the hierarchical management model endowed both these leaders with explicit unilateral authority to command and control. For Blockbuster, Antioco's decision would prove fatal. On the other hand, United Airlines used the lessons learned from the crash of Flight 173 to radically transform its crew management model. By embracing the Crew Resource Management discipline, United's executives transformed their airline and an entire industry, as all carriers replaced the unilateral control authority of the captain with the collective input of collaborative teams. By following a management model that expands the conscious competence of the cockpit in stressful situations, airline crews are leveraging their collective intelligence to uncover blind spots and make better decisions. This team-based management approach has contributed to a noticeable reduction in accidents and, more importantly, deaths.

KNOWNS AND UNKNOWNS

In 1955, two psychologists, Joseph Luft and Harry Ingham, developed a psychological tool called the Johari Window, which recognizes the importance of self-awareness for improving personal development, interpersonal relationships, and group dynamics. The Johari Window, as shown in Figure 6-1, is a four-quadrant model that compares what individuals know about themselves with what others know about them. Each of the four quadrants identifies personal attributes, attitudes, and whether that information is known or unknown to oneself or others.

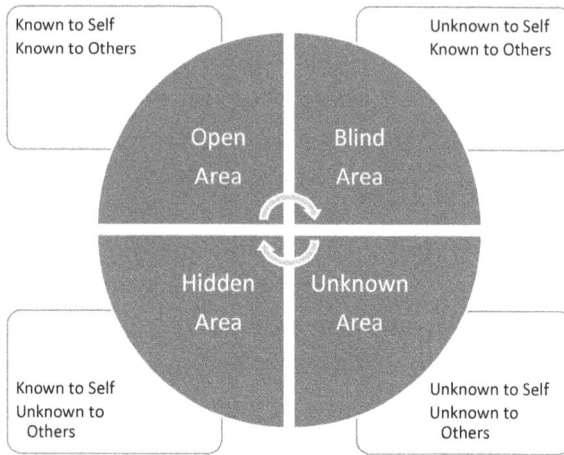

Figure 6-1. Johari Window

The first quadrant is called the Open Area and includes what is known by individuals about themselves and also known by others. The second quadrant, the Blind Area, contains what is unknown by individuals but known by others around them. The third quadrant is labeled the Hidden Area and specifies what individuals know about themselves that others don't know. Finally, the fourth quadrant, the Unknown Area, is a space that represents what is unknown by individuals about themselves and unknown by others.

What is interesting about this model is the only space where there is mutual awareness is the first quadrant. Although the second quadrant is labeled as the Blind Area, to some extent, each of the remaining quadrants contains blind spots where individuals or others around them are unaware of existing attributes or attitudes. This lack of awareness can lead to insufficient information, communication issues, poor decision-making, and a lack of effective coordination among groups.

The Johari Window has become particularly popular among work teams as a tool for improving group dynamics by expanding the Open Area and minimizing the other three quadrants. Through facilitated training activities, members of teams are encouraged to share information about themselves and provide feedback about others in ways that promote a constructive awareness of the strengths and weaknesses of the team.

The Johari Window was one of the tools NASA used when the agency transformed its operating management model from a hierarchy to a network, which we discussed in Chapter 4. In addition to employing the tool to improve individual development and create more effective and collaborative teams, NASA adapted the model as a vehicle to access the state of information as the agency tackled the complex challenges of space travel. In this context, the agency compared what they knew, which they called knowns, with what they didn't know or unknowns.[2] Figure 6-2 presents the adapted model.

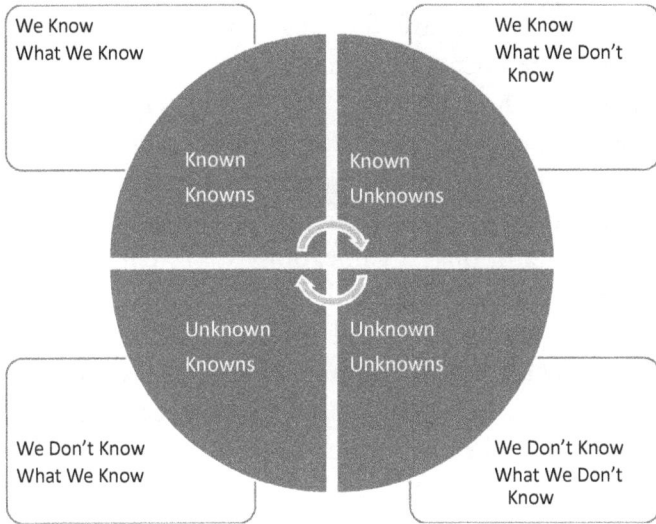

We Know
What We Know

We Know
What We Don't
Know

Known
Knowns

Known
Unknowns

Unknown
Knowns

Unknown
Unknowns

We Don't Know
What We Know

We Don't Know
What We Don't
Know

Figure 6-2. NASA's Adaptation of the Johari Window

The first quadrant contains the Known Knowns. These are givens and provide the same kind of congruent awareness as the Johari Window. However, unlike the Johari Window, the second quadrant is not a blind spot because when you are aware of what you don't know, you can hire knowledgeable outside experts who can transfer this knowledge so that a Known Unknown becomes a Known Known.

In the NASA model, the third and fourth quadrants are the blind spots, but these are not equal challenges because the work of discovering unexplored information is very different for each of the two quadrants. Uncovering the latent knowledge of what you don't know that you know is a relatively easier challenge because Unknown Knowns often become Known Knowns through the natural serendipity of effective teamwork. However, discovering what you don't know that you don't know is far more difficult because this critical knowledge is usually revealed through breakthrough thinking, which obviously can be neither planned nor anticipated.

In using this model to access the state of their information, NASA recognized that their greatest knowledge challenge was the Unknown Unknowns. The importance of focusing on this challenge was famously popularized by the former Secretary of State Donald Rumsfeld in a press conference he held after the NASA staff had briefed him on their practical use of the model to expand their conscious competence.

Finding ways to transform Unknown Unknowns into Known Knowns is often the key to successfully solving complex problems. Unfortunately, traditional organizations are ill-equipped to do this important work. That's because the usual linear thinking processes of command-and-control management are woefully inadequate for navigating the landscape of complex adaptive systems.

The imperative to be competent at uncovering the Unknown Unknowns that are inherent attributes of complex problems is another reason why, in the words of General McCrystal, leaders need to be gardeners rather than chess masters. When leaders are gardeners, they cultivate team environments where people apply systems thinking and learn through experimentation to cultivate the breakthroughs that are the hallmarks of organizations that understand that consciousness and competence are the two key ingredients of organizational effectiveness.

Conscious Competence

While there is broad recognition of the importance of competence among traditional organizations, as evidenced by the well-accepted need to develop and measure core competencies at both the individual and organizational levels, there is little, if any, awareness of the significance of consciousness as an enabler of organizational excellence. This lack of awareness results in the blind spots that often plague organizations.

Figure 6-3 presents the Conscious Competence Matrix, a variation of the NASA application of the Johari window that compares consciousness and competence from an organizational perspective. When organizations are competent, they have sufficient knowledge to carry out tasks, solve problems, and deliver results. When organizations are conscious, they are aware of whether or not they have the knowledge to do the job that needs to be done.

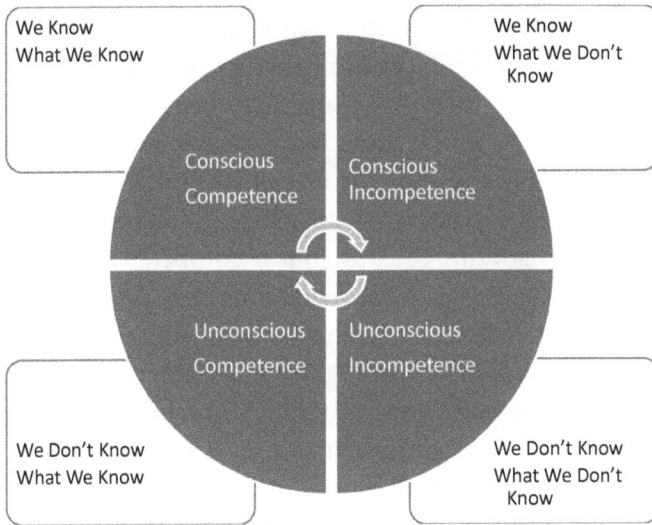

Figure 6-3. Conscious Competence Matrix

The first quadrant is the space of Conscious Competence, where team members have a clear sense of "we know what we know." These are the qualified experienced performers who can confidently rely upon their skills and talents and the known information available to them to plan and execute their work. They know and understand what needs to be done and how to do it.

The second quadrant is Conscious Incompetence. In this space, the team members know what needs to be done, but they also know they don't have the skills or knowledge to do the work. When organizations experience the sense of awareness that "we know what we don't know," they usually bring in outside experts to fill the knowledge gap. Frequently, once this knowledge is brought into the organization, it is easily transferable to the team members and gets added to Conscious Competence going forward.

The third quadrant is an interesting space because it contains skills or information that an organization has but cannot use because this knowledge is outside organizational awareness. This sense of "we don't know what we know" happens when data in organizational systems is not captured in routine reporting structures or when different pieces of critical information are distributed among people in separate departments that don't routinely interact. Put simply, the organization has the knowledge, but decision-makers are unaware and unable to apply the skills or information. Thus, this quadrant is a blind spot and is labeled Unconscious Competence.

The fourth quadrant, Unconscious Incompetence, is a more serious deficiency because the most dangerous risks often happen when organizations are oblivious to the real world because they have no regard for "what we don't know that we don't know." These unknown unknowns render top-down hierarchies' control orientation useless because you can't control things outside your awareness. Often, these unknown unknowns ironically end up in control by triggering the downfall of what was once a highly successful organization. When it came to running a video rental business at scale, John Antioco knew what he knew and performed very well in the space of Conscious Competence. However, when the home entertainment market radically shifted, it was what he didn't know that he didn't know about the future of his industry that would lead to the demise of his business model and, ultimately, his organization.

Most traditional hierarchical organizations operate well in the first two quadrants because qualified performers and external consultants provide the elite intelligence needed when the organization is built around the design principle of trusting authority. However, top-down hierarchies do not operate well in the third or fourth quadrants because they don't have the necessary processes to uncover the unknown knowns or the more troublesome unknown unknowns. One of the key dangers of using a management model that leverages elite intelligence is that experts are prone to hubris. This false sense of certainty is what makes them blind to the possibility of unknown unknowns. It also makes them blind to another flaw of solo decision-makers: unconscious biases.

UNCONSCIOUS BIASES

The human brain is a paradox. While humans can produce highly developed analytical and creative intelligence, they are also prone to make senseless errors. Why is this so? This question sparked the groundbreaking work by the psychologists Daniel Kahneman and Amos Tversky, who studied the psychological dynamics of human decision-making. According to the two psychologists, the answer is that people are nowhere near as rational as they think and are incredibly susceptible to unconscious biases that influence human decision-making to a far greater extent than we realize.

Kahneman and Tversky discovered that people engage in two different thinking modes in their day-to-day lives. They refer to these ways of thinking by the nondescript names System 1 and System 2. System 1 is fast thinking, which operates automatically with little or no effort by using heuristics and templates to navigate the world. System 1 thinking is highly proficient at identifying causal connections between events, sometimes even when there is no empirical basis for the connection. System 2, on the other hand, is slow thinking and involves deliberate attention to understanding details and the complex web of relationships among various components. Whereas System 1 is inherently intuitive, deterministic, and undoubting, System 2 is rational, probabilistic, and highly aware of uncertainty and doubt. Needless to say, these two ways of thinking are contextually very different.

System 1 and System 2 thinking are distinctly human capabilities that have given humanity an immense evolutionary advantage. We can develop complex intellectual structures such as mathematics, physics, and music via applications of System 2, and, thanks to System 1, humans have the unique capability to make judgments and decisions quickly from limited available information. In employing these two capabilities, Kahneman and Tversky found that, while we may perceive ourselves as predominately rational System 2 thinkers, the reality is most human judgments and decisions are based upon the more intuitive System 1 for the simple reason that we don't have the time to do System 2 thinking.

For example, if you suddenly find yourself in an unfamiliar place late at night in the presence of a stranger with no one else in sight, you will need to make some practical decisions rather quickly. Doing a detailed background check on the stranger is impossible, so you will have to quickly judge whether this unknown person is likely friendly, hostile, or indifferent. You will rely upon your experience and intuition to quickly examine the clues in front of you to decide whether to ignore the person, engage in a conversation, or flee as fast as you can.

However, while fast thinking is more useful in making immediate choices, it is also more likely to result in judgment errors, even though we tend to feel more confident when engaged in System 1 than when we employ System 2. That's because the mental narratives that are a natural byproduct of System 1 are likely to result in biases that often cause us to make confident decisions that are completely wrong.

Kahneman and Tversky's research provided clear evidence that most human judgments and decisions—even those by experts—are based on System 1, which means elite authorities are not immune to the hazards of unconscious biases. Often, these biases are swayed by how a problem is initially framed. The two psychologists discovered that how we formulate a situation heavily influences how we decide between alternative courses of action.

Kahneman and Tversky applied the label of "framing effects" to what they described as the unjustified influences of formulation on beliefs and preferences.[3] In a series of experiments, they noticed that people did not choose between things; instead, they chose between descriptions of things. Thus, simply changing the framing—the description of a situation—could cause people to completely flip their attitude on how to respond to the situation.

For example, in an experiment conducted at the Harvard Medical School, Tversky divided physicians into two groups. Each group was given statistics about the five-year survival rates for the outcomes of two treatments for lung cancer: surgery and radiation. While the five-year survival rates were clearly higher for those who received surgery, in the short term, surgery was riskier than radiation. The two groups were then given two different short-term outcome descriptions and asked to choose the preferred treatment. The first group was given the survival rate: The one-month survival rate is 90 percent. The second group was given the corresponding 10 percent mortality rate. Although these two descriptions are logically equivalent, 84 percent of physicians in the first group chose surgery, while the second group was split fifty-fifty between the two options.[4]

If the preferences were completely rational, the physicians would make the same choice regardless of how the descriptions were framed. However, System 1 thinking is not rational and can be swayed by emotional words. Thus, while 90 percent survival sounds promising, 10 percent mortality is shocking. This experiment showed physicians were as vulnerable to the framing effect as hospital patients and business school graduates. As Kahneman observed, "Medical training is, evidently, no defense against the power of framing."[5]

This observation was reinforced by an example that has become known as the "Asian disease problem."[6] Again, the psychologists presented two groups with the same problem:

Imagine that the United States is preparing for the outbreak of an unusual Asian disease, which is expected to kill 600 people.

The first group was asked to choose one of two alternative programs that were framed in terms of how many lives would be saved:

If program A is adopted, 200 people will be saved.

If program B is adopted, there is a one-third probability that 600 people will be saved and a two-thirds probability that no people will be saved.

The second group was asked to choose between two alternative programs that were framed in terms of how many people would die:

If program A is adopted, 400 people will die.

If program B is adopted, there is a one-third probability that nobody will die and a two-thirds probability that 600 people will die.

Once again, the two framings were logically equivalent, and the expectations for each program presented were exactly the same. Nevertheless, Kahneman and Tversky consistently found that the overwhelming majority of respondents in the first group chose program A, while the substantial majority in the second group chose program B.

We might be tempted to conclude that all this experiment proves is the importance of leaving these types of decisions to the experts. Tversky was able to test this assumption when he was invited to give a speech and had the opportunity to do this experiment at a meeting of public health professionals.[7] Once again, half the participants received the lives-saved options and the others received the lives-lost alternatives. Like previous respondents, the public health experts were just as prone to the framing effect.

This troubled Kahneman, who noted, "It is somewhat worrying that the officials who make decisions that affect everyone's health can be swayed by such a superficial manipulation—but we must get used to the idea that even important decisions are influenced, if not governed, by System 1."[8]

The prime contribution of Kahneman and Tversky's lifelong work is to convincingly demonstrate that, when it comes to human decision-making, System 1 is the default mode. Although we may perceive ourselves as thoughtful, rational decision-makers, the evidence says otherwise. All of us—even experts who profess to be data driven—are susceptible to forming cognitive illusions if our conclusions are based on limited evidence.

THE LIMITATIONS OF THE SINGLE BRAIN

At its root, intelligence is the ability to solve problems. We find various degrees of intelligence in all forms of organic life: Microscopic organisms perform elemental tasks. Plants are capable of photosynthesis. Animals develop basic survival skills, and humans create tools to build sophisticated civilizations. As organisms become more complex, the capacity for intelligence increases with each evolutionary leap. This is especially evident with the emergence of the brain, first in animals with relatively primitive proficiencies and ultimately in humans with more fully developed and extraordinary aptitudes. As brains have evolved, they have exponentially increased their problem-solving capacity.

Human intelligence is generally defined as the ability to learn, understand, and make judgments and decisions that are based on reason. However, this definition is more aspirational than factual because it incorrectly implies that System 2 is the default thinking mode. The evidence that the judgments and decisions of the vast majority of people are governed by the intuitive, nonrational, and prone-to-bias System 1 is so compelling that Kahneman was awarded the Nobel Prize in economics for disproving the discipline's fundamental principle that humans are rational decision-makers.

While Taylor's Scientific Management may have intended to provide us with a highly rational management model, the reality is that top-down management has a troublesome design flaw because it amplifies the unconscious and often nonrational biases of an elite few. Given the evidence that System 1 is the default thinking mode, it calls into question the continuing viability of the top-down hierarchical management model, especially as the problems confronting business leaders are becoming exponentially more complex.

Kahneman and Tversky's research also demonstrated that the human brain is not naturally inclined to solve complex problems because people have difficulty mentally managing multiplicity. They found that most people can only handle thinking about two or three things at a time.[9] Accordingly, we easily think associatively, which is the process of linking one thought or idea to another. We think metaphorically when we say that one thing is like another. We naturally think causally whenever we conclude that one thing causes another thing to happen, sometimes even when there is no empirical basis to support the connection. System 1 is compatible with and designed for these forms of linear thinking.

When organizations are designed around the principle of trusting authority, they are constrained by the limitations of the single human brain. Thus, the thinking capacity of the organization is limited by the thinking capacity of the elite few who are invested with coercive power. Because command-and-control dynamics generally preclude the practical ability of subordinates to overrule the judgments of authorities, management activity tends to be restricted to the known concerns of the elite leaders, which are the areas of Conscious Competence and Conscious Incompetence in Figure 6-3. These two areas are the domain of Taylor's Scientific Management.

When elites are to be trusted and never challenged, questioning authority is often considered insubordination rather than an opportunity for learning or expanding the organization's consciousness. This is problematic because the more rational System 2 thinking dynamics involve raising questions, exploring uncertainties, and parsing ambiguities. These are the same dynamics necessary for navigating the areas of Unconscious Competence and Unconscious Incompetence. However, because System 1's simplistic linear thinking often results in a misplaced sense of overconfidence, the unfortunate consequence of entrusting elite leaders with coercive power is that management lacks the capacity for working in these two critical areas, which renders organizations incapable of solving complex problems.

When management lacks the capacity to access and leverage the collective intelligence of the entire organization and is restrained by the thinking capacity of the single human brains of an elite few, they create severe learning disabilities that diminish the intelligence of the entire organization. By design, top-down hierarchies are low-intelligence organizations because they are constrained by linear thinking and prone to amplify the biases of System 1 thinking, especially the bias to maintain the status quo. Consequently, leaders will often propagate unconsciously biased framings of situations reinforced through coercive uniformity of thought, which can lead to senseless decisions. These decisions often emanate from cause-and-effect conclusions that have no basis in reality despite obvious signs that are usually hiding in plain sight. System 1 thinking tends to assume what we see is all there is and, thus, prevents leaders from uncovering the blind spots that can lead to their organizations' demise.

EXTRAORDINARILY INTELLIGENT ORGANIZATIONS

If business leaders want to avoid the hazards of System 1 thinking, they will need to embrace the notion that the critical work of management is not about the expansion of control but the expansion of consciousness. They will need to become highly adept at working in all four quadrants of the Conscious Competence Matrix because that is the domain of System 2 thinking.

This will be a challenge because working in all four quadrants means transforming centralized, top-down hierarchies into self-managed, peer-to-peer networks and embracing the holistic tools and practices of systems thinking.

Systems thinking does not come naturally to hierarchical leaders because it requires them to think holistically about many things simultaneously. Most people—even highly educated people—have difficulty thinking holistically. Systems thinking recognizes that what you see is not all there is, understands reality is probabilistic rather than deterministic, and, when done well, naturally produces more comprehensive solutions that are less likely to result in unintended consequences.

Systems thinking is hard work because it requires us to learn what we need to know to formulate a solution rather than to assume, based on our experience, that we already know what needs to be done. Thinking holistically involves deliberate attention to understanding the complex web of relationships among the various components of a problem and recognizing that some of those components are beyond our areas of expertise.

The solutions to complex problems are always holistic and usually require the balanced input of a diverse team of people bringing multiple perspectives. In other words, no single person has the insight to solve complex problems because the solutions are beyond the limitations of the single human brain. When this is the case, management's critical work is clearly about expanding organizational consciousness and not personal control. Accordingly, solving complex problems requires the capacity to tap into the collective intelligence of a network of brains.

Cultivating systems thinking means the basic units of organizations are cross-functional teams that behave like a network of brains by welcoming diversity of opinion, respecting all voices, encouraging independent thinking, and integrating the best of everyone's ideas to create solutions that no single individual could accomplish alone. These are the behaviors that enable organizations to make the leap from low to extraordinary intelligence.

A core corollary of the design principle that nobody is smarter than everybody is that there is nothing more powerful than getting the whole system in the same space at the same time. This is the key dynamic for transforming a group of individuals into a network of brains where the whole is greater than the sum of the parts. As the team goes about the work of solving problems, each member can react in real time to the comments and observations of the other members. Because no single person on the team has coercive power to silence or overrule another member, the team has to engage in conversations that consider all points of view to find solutions that work for everyone in the group. These conversations are the catalysts that enable teams to uncover what they didn't know they already knew as different team members share perspectives that enhance the understanding of the whole group. More importantly, getting everybody in the same space at the same time is often the best vehicle for discovering what they don't know that they don't know, as one group learned in a collective intelligence workshop I facilitated a few years back.

The company involved was transitioning between two vendors to service a critical customer information portal. With less than ninety days to the handover and indications that the transition was in serious trouble, I was asked to facilitate a collective intelligence workshop to see what could be done to rescue the project. The one-day session brought together forty individuals from the different organizational units that were involved in the transition.

As people arrived before the workshop started, I noticed that one individual was obviously not happy to be a part of the session. His body language conveyed that, with all the pressure he was feeling to deliver what appeared to be an impossible task, he did not have the time to attend an all-day meeting. Throughout most of the day, as we continued our work through a cadence of small group exercises and large group discussions, I noticed his obvious displeasure. By the end of the day, the group had identified four critical activities that were the keys to a successful transition. As I reviewed the day's work before ending the session, it was clear that most of the group members felt a sense of relief that they had identified the roadmap to a smooth handover. When I asked if anyone had any final comments, the person who seemed to be unhappy raised his hand. He commented that when he was told he had to attend this session, he was quite annoyed because he expected the meeting would be a complete waste of time. He told the group he was very wrong and that this was one of the best meetings he had ever attended. He then pointed to a flip chart containing the key steps for one of the four critical activities the group had identified. He commented that it was not just an important activity but the most important thing the group needed to do to ensure a smooth transition. He continued to

113

say that before walking into the meeting, he and everyone else in the room weren't even aware of the need for this activity.

By getting everyone in the same space at the same time, we had created the conditions for the group to uncover what they didn't know they didn't know and to move from low to extraordinary intelligence. With this intelligence, they could accomplish a completely successful on-time transition.

The collective intelligence workshop is one way traditional organizations can experience the extraordinary intelligence that comes more naturally to self-managed organizations. Because no one in the workshop has the authority to silence or coerce another person, the group is far less likely to experience the blind spots that pervade low-intelligence hierarchical organizations. When people are free to express inconvenient truths or dissenting points of view and the dynamics of the conversation support the deep understanding of all points of view—regardless of agreement or disagreement—unconscious biases can be uncovered. The possibility of real learning that expands the consciousness of the whole group becomes a powerful source for identifying innovative ways of solving complex problems.

Unless all voices are heard and respected, organizations cannot solve complex problems because the key to tackling these wicked issues is often the resolution of a paradox, which generally means two apparently contradictory objectives must be met.

Hierarchies don't handle paradoxes well because they are naturally inclined to fall into the trap of either/or thinking. When this happens, conversations tend to devolve into debates around which objective is more important. By pitting the two objectives against each other, the likely resolution will be the selection of one over the other. Once the decision is made, it's likely that dissent will no longer be tolerated, even though the objections may be sound. This is one of the key dynamics that destroys worker engagement. Avoiding this dynamic is what Bill Gore had in mind when he built his self-managed organization around the fundamental notion that no single person would have the authority to kill a good idea or keep a bad idea alive.

Peer-to-peer networks handle paradoxes far better by embracing both/and rather than either/or thinking, as happened in another collective intelligence workshop I facilitated with the Blue Cross Blue Shield Federal Employee Program (FEP). We had gathered approximately fifty people, representing a microcosm of our organization, to assess our progress in making critical software updates to our claims processing system. As the workshop proceeded, we found ourselves confronted with an uncomfortable paradox. While the operations staff had identified additional systems updates necessary to ensure a satisfactory customer service experience, the systems staff was pushing back, saying there wasn't sufficient time to accommodate the updates. As I listened to the two different points of view, it was clear that both perspectives were sound. I remember thinking we had encountered the proverbial "indestructible object that had met the immovable force."

One of the great advantages of collective intelligence workshops is that, with everyone in the same space at the same time, they provide better opportunities for quickly solving apparently intractable problems. With this in mind, I instructed the participants, who were seated around six tables, to see if they could identify a solution that would satisfy the concerns of the two perspectives. After thirty minutes in their small group discussions, each table reported out their ideas. One of the tables suggested we might resolve the problem if we postponed another project the systems staff was doing that was completely unrelated to the problematic systems update. With a microcosm of the business in the room, I could ask the group if there would be any harm if we followed the table's suggestion. When everyone agreed that we could easily live with postponing the other systems project, I asked the systems staff if they could now perform the additional systems updates. When they replied yes, we had resolved our paradox and found a both/and solution.

This is an example of how gathering everyone in the same space at the same time can move a group past the limitations of System 1 thinking to the more thorough System 2. In addition, by having the capability to leverage the collective intelligence of the large group, we were able to do System 2 thinking at System 1 speeds. This represents an extraordinary leap in organizational intelligence and is the great advantage that networks leveraging the collective intelligence of the many have over hierarchies amplifying the intelligence of the elite few. No single individual can do System 2 thinking at System 1 speeds. Only a diverse network of people who are free to express their opinions without fear of coercion or retaliation can accomplish that feat.

Three Dimensions of an Organization

All organizations have three fundamental dimensions: intelligence, power, and performance. As previously mentioned, intelligence is the ability to solve problems. Power is the capacity to take action, and performance is the wherewithal to accomplish results. A highly effective organization is competent in all three dimensions. One out of three or two out of three is not good enough to sustain continued success. A well-crafted strategy without the people and the resources to deliver is nothing more than wishful thinking, as many failed startups have painfully learned. Doing the wrong thing right is operational excellence that no longer results in sales, as Kodak discovered when digital photography displaced film processing.

In this chapter, we have focused on intelligence and how the evolutionary shift in the nature of problems from complicated to complex issues requires new ways of thinking to solve today's more wicked challenges. Conventional intelligence, reductionist thinking, and reliance on the historical expertise of individual experts, which have been the longstanding habits of top-down hierarchies, are woefully inadequate in solving the unprecedented problems of a rapidly changing and increasingly complex world. Complex problems can only be solved holistically by leveraging the collective intelligence of whole teams and employing the unfamiliar tools and practices of human systems thinking. In short, this evolutionary shift in the nature of problems requires a leap to a more highly evolved form of human intelligence that is free from the unconscious biases of the select few and able to leverage the collective wisdom of the many to uncover critical unknowns and expand the consciousness of the whole organization. When it comes to solving complex problems, nobody really is smarter than everybody.

In the next chapter, we will turn our attention to the second organizational dimension and discuss why and how the changing nature of problems requires not just an extraordinary leap in intelligence but, more importantly, a radical transformation in how power works in organizations.

7

WHEN POWER DOES NOT CORRUPT

During the first semester of my junior year in college, I learned a valuable lesson about power that would permanently shape my management practice. On the first day of a class in social psychology, the professor surprised me—and I'm sure many of the other 200 students in the room—by informing us that we would not be required to attend any of the lectures for the rest of the semester. There would only be two requirements that would affect our grades. Half of our marks would be based on the average of our mid-term and final exams. The other half would be based upon our participation in a two-day simulated society exercise, which would be held on a weekend in October.

The professor told the students that the lectures and exams would not contain any material not in the assigned readings. So, if we felt comfortable that we could master the content of the readings on our own, there was no need to attend the lectures. However, everyone would be required to attend the weekend event. There would be no exceptions. The professor emphasized if there was a family wedding we had to attend on that weekend, we needed to drop the course because anyone who missed the simulated society exercise would get an F for the activity and would fail the course.

The professor then described the grading approach. While the exam scores would be individually calculated for each person in the class, everyone in the simulated society would receive the same score based on the group's performance in the exercise. Because the ideal size is one hundred students, the class would be divided into two groups. Thus, each group would have its own score. The professor also encouraged anyone who found this grading approach unacceptable to drop the course.

In preparation for the October weekend, we were given questionnaires that would be used to assign social roles to the various participants in each of the two simulated societies. I remember one question in particular because I thought long and hard about how to answer the item. I needed to choose which of three attributes motivated me the most: achievement, affiliation, or power. As I thought about the three choices, I felt the most socially acceptable answers would be either achievement or affiliation. That's because if people strive to be successful at an art or craft, we think of them as wanting to be accomplished, or if individuals are good at making friends, we call them popular. However, if people are driven by a need for power, we often describe them as controlling or manipulative. Most of us tend to think of power in a negative light. Nevertheless, as I grappled with how to respond to this question, I knew my honest answer was power. Although I felt an internal pressure to select the more acceptable attributes, I ultimately chose what really motivated me most and selected power.

AN ENLIGHTENING WEEKEND

When the October weekend arrived, the two groups were directed to their separate facilities for the exercise, and each person was assigned a social role. My position was to serve as the chief justice for the society, which meant I led the group that had the authority to determine whether actions or proposed actions of individuals or groups would violate the rules of the society. I immediately suspected that my response to the motivation question influenced my selection for this role.

The simulated society began with a basic overview of the exercise and its rules by a small team of monitors. They would be with us for the weekend to observe the society's activities, answer questions about the exercise, and ensure the participants were adhering to the rules of the simulation. The facility had four rooms, known as regions, with one-quarter of the group assigned to each room. Our ability to move between regions was restricted in two ways. First, depending on one's assigned role or designated region, some individuals could move more freely between rooms. Others were restricted to a very limited number of transits between the regions. Second, at no time could more than 50 percent of the society be physically present in any region.

The rights and responsibilities of the various roles were also explained. These included a president of the society, other governmental agents, political party members, industry leaders, employees, and media journalists. We were also given an overview of the society's money supply, how it worked, and how it was initially distributed among the participants. Throughout the weekend, we would be presented with various social problems that we would need to solve by coordinating activities and transferring resources across the society. Failure to adequately solve these problems could lead to poor industrial production, unemployment of members, or even the "deaths" of some participants. The basic challenge of the exercise was to balance the individual and group needs of different components of our society. At various times throughout the exercise, the progress of different social aspects would be measured and reported to all the participants.

After the overview was complete and the participants had moved to their assigned rooms, the simulated society began. We weren't too long into the exercise before I noticed that, even though this was a game, some participants became seriously self-involved in their roles and were jockeying to advance their societal standing. They seemed determined to promote their positions without regard for the common good as we were presented with social problems, such as food shortages in one of the regions. In particular, these individuals seemed willing to exploit the communication challenges created by the dispersion of the society to advance their positions.

I also noticed early in the exercise that several people were more concerned with focusing on the society's overall health, even if it meant they needed to dispense with some of their personally assigned resources. One of those participants was the president of the society. Recognizing we were like-minded, he and I quickly formed an alliance. We agreed we would use the power that came with our positions to enable—to the extent we could—an optimal balance of the needs of individual participants and the society overall. In particular, we would do all we could to ensure that no group or individual could expand their wealth at the expense of others, and we would support the enrichment of any group or individual that contributed to society's overall health. We also agreed we would use our influence to minimize the accumulation of centralized power by either the society's governmental agents or industry leaders. This meant doing our best to ensure that the government served the people rather than the people being made accountable to the government. It also meant all the industries flourished with none accumulating monopoly power, participants remained employed in their jobs, and no one died. Through executive action that the rules provided for the president's role and the judicial rulings incumbent on my position, the two of us and other like-minded leaders could promote win-win strategies to accomplish a healthy balance between group and individual needs.

By Saturday afternoon, it was clear that the win-win strategies were working, and an esprit-de-corps was emerging. This was reflected in favorable measures for the individual industries and overall society. Throughout Sunday morning, social cohesion continued growing as the participants collaborated to successfully resolve new issues in the game. It was clear that most, if not all, of the participants were having a good learning experience and a fun time.

Things were going so well that, early Sunday afternoon, one of the participants devised an interesting proposal that required a judicial opinion. Although we had been divided into four regions, we were actually in two physical rooms on opposite sides of a hall that had been partitioned into four rooms using movable walls. The proposal was to assemble the society into two regions on one side of the hall, with half the society in each adjacent room, and open the movable partition so we could close the weekend with a party for the whole society.

After examining the rules, our judicial team couldn't find anything that prohibited this action, so we ruled in favor of the proposal. The monitors immediately objected and advised us we couldn't make this ruling. I asked them to show us where the rules specifically said the partitions couldn't be moved. They begrudgingly admitted this wasn't addressed in the rules. The monitors then asked if we would agree to postpone the opinion for twenty minutes so they could check with the professor who was at the second facility observing the other simulated society. We agreed, and fifteen minutes later, the professor walked into the room, informed us that we could move back the partition, and announced that we could go ahead with our party after we spent thirty minutes reflecting on our weekend experience.

The professor opened the reflection by congratulating the group for a job well done in building a highly cohesive society, which he noted happens in less than 5 percent of the groups participating in this exercise. To the delight of everyone, he announced that each participant would receive an A for this half of our course grade. The professor noted he needed to hurry back to the other society after our group reflection because they were having a more typical experience.

The valuable lesson I learned from this weekend is when the basis for exercising power is more about *power with* rather than *power over*, groups of diverse individuals with different needs and resources can find ways to solve difficult problems that work for the large majority of a group. In other words, there are circumstances where power does not corrupt. It is the drive for power over others or the coercive power that is endemic to centralized hierarchies that is inherently corrupt because it divides groups into the powerful and powerless. A preference for power with others does not corrupt because no one is inherently powerless, and every individual in the group can work together to create something greater than any one of them could devise on their own.

This lesson would prove valuable once again over two decades later when, as discussed in Chapter 3, I was asked to turn around the operations of the Blue Cross Blue Shield Federal Employee Program (FEP) and chose to invest in power with others by using a network-based management model to accomplish the job.

TRANSFORMING HOW POWER WORKS

The greatest distinction between centralized, top-down hierarchies and self-managed, peer-to-peer networks is the way power works in these markedly different organizational models. That's because these two different models tap into radically different aspects of power. In hierarchies, power belongs to those in charge. Thus, the capacity to take action belongs to an elite few who are invested with command-and-control authority over subordinates expected to follow the direction and orders of their supervisors.

The integral dynamic for how power works in top-down organizations is coercive power, which means bosses can legitimately exercise force to cause employees to behave in ways they would otherwise not choose. Accordingly, coercive power uses fear and control to keep employees compliant. When power over people is the prevailing practice for getting things done, it fosters a work environment where the small number at the top feel powerful, and the vast majority of workers see themselves as powerless. Perhaps this explains why, according to the Deloitte Shift Index, 80 percent of people are dissatisfied with their jobs.[1]

On the other hand, in self-managed networks, power belongs to the connected. The more people you are connected to, the more powerful you are, and the more connections there are among team members, the more powerful the team is. In networks, because there are no bosses or subordinates, everyone is considered a contributor and has the capacity to take action. This is the practice at Buurtzorg where, without bosses, the voices of all nurses on a team matter. Everyone can share their ideas on how to organize and perform their work, and the distribution of tasks is mutually agreed upon by all team members.

In self-managed networks, the exercise of coercive power is non-existent because no single individual has power over another. The source of power in networks is derived from a very different aspect of power. Rather than employing force to get things done, the source of power in networks is *energy*.

In physics, energy is the ability to do work. In self-managed networks, the ability to do work is accomplished through the emergent energy that flows from the interaction of teams of collegial contributors who combine the best of their ideas and skills to achieve extraordinary performance. This emergent energy is synergistic power. When organizations fully invest in power with people by honoring all voices, encouraging diversity of opinion, and leveraging the collective intelligence of everyone on their various teams to solve the problems and paradoxes of delivering the business, they create a powerful enterprise far greater than the sum of its parts.

Organizations that leverage synergistic power have a distinct competitive advantage in the marketplace. That's because self-managed networks are designed to engage in the iterative discovery that enables team members to rise above their innate biases and learn from each other. This knowledge enables organizational networks to adapt more quickly to changing circumstances than their hierarchical counterparts, whose employees are often powerless to change course because unconscious biases blind a stubborn individual leader.

Because synergistic power is energy, it cannot be confined to certain individuals or levels. All voices matter, and all relationships are collegial. According to Margaret Wheatley, author of *Leadership and the New Science*, "When power is shared in such workplace designs as participative management and self-managed teams, positive creative power abounds."[2] This positive energy is what makes synergistic power far more effective than coercive power for accomplishing the work of an organization.

It's important to note that engaging in synergistic power does not mean you always get what you want. However, it does mean you will always have a voice, and your voice will be heard. There is no censorship or manipulation of information in peer-to-peer networks. Unlike top-down hierarchies that silence dissenting voices to promote uniformity of thought to "get everybody on the same page," networks welcome diversity of opinion because it's a far more effective path to mutual agreements that will work. Even though you may not get your way after you've been heard, as long as the group's solution works, most people will agree to go along, as happened in a collective intelligence workshop I facilitated when I was with Blue Cross Blue Shield FEP.

In 2006, the federal government decided to supplement the health insurance program it had offered since 1960 with separate programs to provide dental and vision benefits for federal workers. While we were working to develop our proposal for the dental product, a difficult issue emerged that almost derailed our efforts to offer a dental benefit. The particular sticking point involved the design of a new insurance claims processing model to coordinate benefits between the central processor of the existing health product, which was located in one of the Blue Cross Blue Shield organizations, and the central processor for the new proposed dental product, which was to be resident in another Blue Cross Blue Shield company. Each of the two central processors proposed very different models for coordinating benefits between them, and each passionately advocated its model. Because of speed-to-market requirements, selecting one of these was critical to moving the project forward. Recognizing the only decision that would work was one that all parties could support, we convened a collective intelligence workshop of thirty-five participants representing all areas involved in the project to resolve this critical issue.

On the meeting day, we opened the workshop with presentations of the proposed models from each of the two processors. Each presentation was delivered without interruption, followed by a period of clarifying questions to make sure everyone fully understood each approach. When the presentations and questions were completed, I divided the thirty-five participants into four small table groups. I asked each group to select one of the two models and to list the top three to four reasons for that selection. After forty-five minutes in the small group discussions, each table reported its results with all four tables selecting the health product processor's model for reasons that were obviously consistent across the four groups.

I observed a clear consensus for using the health processor's model when all the small group reports were complete. Everyone in the room nodded in apparent agreement. To be certain that a true consensus had been reached, I asked the participants, "Is there anyone in the room who cannot live with this selection?" I cautioned the group that no one should agree just for the sake of going along, nor should anyone hang onto a preference out of stubbornness. However, if there was anyone who truly believed the selected approach would fail and, thus, could not live with the selection, that individual needed to come forward. We needed to understand his or her concerns. Sometimes, one person sees something that the rest of the group does not, and that insight might very well move the group in a different direction. This is why it is so important to honor all voices. Consensus is not about the majority ruling; instead, it's about identifying the optimal workable solution everyone can live with.

In response to this final question, all thirty-five participants—including those who initially advocated the model that was not selected—agreed they could live with and support the group's decision. With true consensus and agreement achieved, the project could move forward. Because we took the time to gather the whole system in one place and could access and leverage the group's collective intelligence, we could craft an effective, shared understanding that was far more acceptable than a command decision. Even though the staff from the dental processor did not get their way in how benefits would be coordinated with the health processor, they went along with the clear preference of the majority in the workshop because they were fully heard.

Who Decides?

As FEP's chief executive, I had the formal authority to decide which processing model to use. However, because I had chosen to lead FEP using a peer-to-peer network management system rather than the traditional command-and-control model, I was committed to the principle of sharing power with people rather than exercising power over them in making this critical decision. The important lesson I learned in college taught me the decisions that emerge from building shared understanding among divergent interests work better than command directions from a single leader. Over the years, I learned this is true for two key reasons.

First, as smart as leaders may be, they are still limited in their understanding by the boundaries of their individual experience and, more importantly, by their unconscious biases. This was clearly evident when John Antioco unilaterally decided to pass on the opportunity to buy Netflix because he was convinced online video would have no impact on his business model. In his mind, the internet craze was completely overblown. Surely, there were people inside Blockbuster who understood how the internet would transform their industry. If the video company had engaged in a process like the collective intelligence workshop, those other voices would have been heard. Blockbuster would likely have made a better decision that would have paved the way to successfully adapt to a radically changing market.

Second, when employees know their voices matter and can participate in decision-making, they become highly engaged. By having the freedom to meaningfully influence decisions, they help craft better outcomes and gain a solid understanding of how everyone on various work teams is affected by decisions. In addition, they gain an appreciation for the diverse skills among their team members and a comforting sense that people know what they are doing. This last point is important because high engagement flows from this sense of common competence and fuels synergistic power.

This sharply contrasts traditional siloed organizations, where most employees feel their voices don't matter. There is no joy in following orders that often don't make sense. Additionally, should people try to suggest a better way, they are admonished to do what they're told because the decision has already been made. These employees often have deep feelings of isolation because they typically do not understand how their contributions fit with others. As a result, they often have the sense that nobody in the organization really knows what they are doing. This sense is the primary cause of the high levels of disengagement in top-down hierarchies.

The most important question that shapes what kind of organization you will build is: *Who decides?* All the key attributes that define the fundamental structure of your organization flow from your answer to this most important question. Should you decide that a designated managerial group will be responsible for decision-making, your organization will be based on the design principle of trusting authority. Accordingly, you will invest decision-making authority with an elite corps of managers arrayed into a hierarchy of bosses. The most senior of these managers will be individually responsible for leading specific functions and endowed with the authority to make unilateral decisions for their areas of responsibility. As a group, these senior leaders will be responsible for centrally planning business strategy.

The remaining bosses will serve as middle managers who will be distributed among the functional areas and given command-and-control authority over the subordinate employees who report to them. In addition, information will be distributed among people on a need-to-know basis. Once decisions are made, conformity with the organization's ideology and compliance with the directives of management will be considered the pathways to high performance. Failure to conform and comply—or even raise objections—after decisions are made will be viewed as insubordination and may even be grounds for dismissal from the organization. Entrusting decision-making to an elite few will inevitably lead to coercive force as the basis for exercising power within the organization.

On the other hand, should you decide—as Chris Rufer did when he and his colleagues built Morning Star's organization—that everyone is a manager and all members of work teams should be involved in making decisions, your organization will be based on the design principle that nobody is smarter than everybody. Thus, your organizational attributes will support the essential activity of aggregating and leveraging collective intelligence. There will be no bosses because no one will have coercive authority to exert their will over another person or group. Information will flow freely because everyone in a peer-to-peer network needs access to critical data and knowledge of important developments to participate intelligently in decision-making. Recognizing that collating collective intelligence is only possible if all colleagues are free to express their thinking without fear of retaliation, diversity of opinion will be encouraged and welcomed by organizing into a collection of small, cross-functional, collegial teams. These teams will be responsible for making decisions and determining how decisions will be made. Rather than following a fixed set of plans and directives from superiors, the strategy will emerge and evolve from the iterative discovery that is a natural byproduct of an organization designed for rapid, adaptive learning precisely because all voices matter. Collegial agreement rather than enforced compliance will be the social dynamic driving high performance. Placing decision-making in the hands of teams who do the actual work will accelerate the high energy that is the signature of synergistic power.

AUTONOMY AND SHARED UNDERSTANDING

Although it may seem counterintuitive to traditional leaders, the more freedom individuals are given to make decisions, the more orderly the organization is. However, individual freedom is not absolute. Self-management is not a free-for-all but the aligned actions of autonomous individuals operating within a context of a shared understanding. Reed Hastings, the cofounder of Netflix, relates a powerful example of how the combination of autonomous action and shared understanding can make a big difference.[3]

Between 2013 and 2018, one of the most-watched television series was the political thriller *House of Cards*. Netflix made a huge bet their customers would embrace a streaming series that would release all episodes of a season on a single day, allowing viewers to watch the series on their schedules. At the time, Samsung had just introduced the new ultra-high-definition 4K TV, and Netflix had invested a sizable amount of money to produce the series to be compatible with this new video technology. However, these new TVs were expensive, and the staff members at Netflix weren't sure people would buy them.

Nigel Baptiste, the director of partner engagement, was convinced if people experienced the high quality of 4K viewing, they would pay the premium for this superior technology. He partnered with the staff at Samsung to see what they could do to pique people's interest in this new TV format. They contacted the *Washington Post* journalist Geoffrey Fowler, who reviews high-tech products for the two million readers of the popular newspaper, and he agreed to see a test demonstration of *House of Cards* on Samsung's new TV. The test viewing was scheduled for a Friday at 10:00 a.m.

On the Thursday before the demonstration, Netflix's engineers did a dry run to ensure that Fowler would have an extraordinary viewing experience. With everything working properly, the Netflix staff went home looking forward to the Friday preview. However, when Baptiste arrived at the office on Friday morning at 8:15 a.m., he was stunned to discover the 4K TV was gone. It was mistakenly hauled away by Netflix facilities staff on Thursday evening, along with several old TVs previously scheduled for disposal. With less than two hours before the demonstration and no time to procure another 4K TV, this incredible opportunity for a positive review that could reach millions of people appeared lost. As Baptiste hung his head in despair, thinking he was out of options to rescue the preview, a junior engineer ran into his office to tell him all was well. The engineer had stopped by the office late Thursday night and saw the 4K TV had been taken away. Realizing how important this demonstration was, he attempted to contact Baptiste. When he didn't get a response to his calls and texts, the engineer took the initiative, bought a 4K TV at a local Best Buy, brought it back to the office, and tested it. "It cost $2,500," he said, "But I thought it was the right thing to do."[4]

Baptiste was both elated and floored by the actions of the junior engineer. He knew, in the typical company, a junior employee would never feel comfortable taking this kind of initiative. At that moment, he appreciated Netflix's unusual approach to responsible decision-making. All the people involved in the Netflix 4K TV demonstration had a shared understanding of the importance of obtaining a positive review that could reach millions of people. When the junior engineer couldn't contact the project lead, he didn't throw up his hands and think it was too bad there was nothing he could do because he didn't have the authority to approve this purchase. Instead, the shared understanding he learned by being part of this team guided him in making an autonomous decision that he knew was the right thing to do.

Decision-making works better in self-managed networks than in top-down hierarchies because networks provide the tools and processes for everyone to exercise intelligent judgment. By leveraging collective intelligence to process information among cross-functional teams, networks provide a sense of clarity rarely seen in traditional organizations in the form of a shared understanding that allows anyone in any situation to make intelligent decisions in critical moments. Individual autonomy in the context of a shared understanding allows the people in self-managed networks to make smarter and faster decisions, which is exactly what happened when a junior engineer made a late-night decision to buy a $2,500 TV for his company. This explains why researchers at Cornell University found businesses that granted workers autonomy grew at four times the rate of traditional control-oriented companies and had one-third the turnover.[5]

How Decisions Are Made

Just as there are operating protocols for making decisions in top-down hierarchies, there are tools and practices that govern decision-making in self-managed networks. Once again, peer-to-peer networks are not disjointed free-for-alls where anything goes. The decision-making processes of networks are products of specific norms designed to ensure that no individual can dominate the group's thinking by talking over others, disrespecting alternative viewpoints, intimidating members of the team, or speaking incessantly. The meetings of self-managed teams are places where participants feel safe to express their thinking and where all members have a balanced involvement to ensure everyone is heard. These meetings work best when a designated facilitator is responsible for the safety and balance of the group discussion, as is the practice at Buurtzorg.

Buurtzorg's distributed decision-making architecture follows a simple set of protocols. When a team gathers for a meeting, the first thing the group does is choose a facilitator. The facilitator's role is to serve as a gardener, cultivating a productive discussion that helps the team reach decisions that work for all members. Accordingly, the facilitator can only ask questions or summarize what others have contributed to the discussion. By accepting the role of facilitator, the individual agrees not to advocate for any particular outcome.

After a facilitator is selected, the meeting proceeds through a series of rounds. The first round is the construction of the agenda. As each person contributes a proposal, the item is listed on a flip chart. If the item is not self-evident, the facilitator may ask the contributor to provide the rationale for the proposed agenda. During this round, there is no open discussion. Similar to the table reports in collective intelligence workshops, which we discussed in Chapter 3, team members are restricted to clarifying questions. If the team is going to build shared understanding, each member needs to appreciate different points of view, regardless of agreement or disagreement.

An open discussion takes place in the second round. This is the space for dialogue and debate on how to handle the item. In this round, team members are free to agree, disagree, and offer alternative ideas or options for resolving an issue. The facilitator ensures that no one or two individuals dominate the discussion and that everyone's voice is heard and respected. Each agenda item is reviewed, improved, and refined as the group exchanges ideas.[6]

Once the group thoroughly understands and fully discusses all the agenda items, the team proceeds into the third round, where decisions are made regarding each issue. The operating principle needed to reach decisions is that nobody has a principled objection.[7] In other words, even though an individual might feel there is a better solution, if that person agrees the decision favored by most will work, the team will proceed with the approach favored by the majority. However, suppose there is a principled reason behind the objection, such as the decision might violate a regulatory requirement. In that case, the majority decision cannot be adopted until that concern is thoroughly examined. Buurtzorg's collegial meeting process can be used by any team that would like to gain experience in self-managed group decision-making.

Another example is a meeting format that W. L. Gore and Associates use to tap into the powerful resource of the company's collective intelligence to decide whether new project ideas will receive funding. Because all work is accepted rather than assigned, associates at Gore are responsible for finding work on an existing team or creating a new team to pursue an innovative idea. While everyone at Gore has the freedom to advance a new business idea, funding for proposals has to be earned by making a credible business case for the market viability of an innovation. Gore provides the opportunity for earning funding by periodically scheduling large group sessions where teams can pitch their ideas to other Gore associates who will decide which proposals have market viability.

These facilitated sessions typically have around fifty attendees and include all members of the pitch teams as well as a sufficient number of other Gore associates. During the session, the facilitator invites each team to present its idea for a fixed time, usually fifteen or twenty minutes. Typically, these presentations detail the elements that are contained in the popular Business Model Canvas, such as value propositions, customer segment analysis, cost structure, expected revenue streams, and identification of key partners, activities, and resources. In addition, attendees are invited to ask questions to better understand each proposal.

When all the presentations are complete, the facilitator gives each attendee a strip of six stick-on dots, which can be applied to a flip chart listing each of the proposals presented in the session. The facilitator informs the group that each dot represents $10,000, and they are to individually decide if they would invest their dots in any of the proposals. The attendees are free to invest as they see fit, including not investing any dots should they think none of the proposals are ready for funding. The one caveat is that members of presenting teams cannot invest in their proposal; they can only apply their dots to the remaining proposals.

When the dots have been applied, the facilitator tallies the results to identify which proposals have received sufficient votes of confidence to be considered for funding. These proposals will be recommended to a separate budget team that will determine the amount of the actual funding.

The session concludes with feedback for proposals not recommended for funding. This candid discussion is an opportunity for teams to learn what they might need to do to improve the readiness of their proposals. This feedback can help guide them in doing the work necessary to earn funding in a future pitch session, or the team may realize that their proposal is not viable and should be abandoned. If this happens, abandonment is not considered a failure because not every idea is expected to succeed. In fact, understanding why a particular idea doesn't work and communicating that understanding across the organization is considered valuable because it often saves what might be wasted effort by other teams considering similar ideas.

One benefit of this decision-making practice is a more efficient process for abandoning failing projects before they consume considerable resources. Far too often, in hierarchical organizations, projects in trouble deplete precious time and resources because leaders feel their personal success and compensation hinge on completing the project. Because the performance metrics of most organizations don't incentivize abandoning initiatives, there is a strong bias to complete a project once it is established, even if market factors or customer feedback indicate a lack of interest.

Because some level of failure is inevitable when innovation is a core value, it is essential to have processes that encourage initiative and fiscal discipline. At Gore, anyone is free to pursue any idea, but funding needs to be earned. Therefore, teams need to demonstrate that their ideas have a practical chance to generate revenue. Colossal failures are less likely to happen in Gore's self-managed structure because there are no bosses who will continue to invest time and money into doomed projects because they view abandonment as an admission of personal failure.

In addition to pitch sessions, Gore uses another simple protocol to determine whether ideas should be pursued or abandoned: Projects begin when enough people come to the meeting, and projects are abandoned when enough people stop showing up. This protocol is a highly efficient market mechanism that helps keep Gore both innovative and profitable.

DECISION BOUNDARIES

Most companies distinguish between two types of decisions: strategic and operating. Strategic decisions are those that represent growth or innovation opportunities that could greatly amplify a firm's market position if successful or severely damage the company if the strategy fails. On the other hand, operating decisions involve coordinating the normal day-to-day operations of the business. How leaders make strategic and operating decisions can vary widely.

In self-managed networks, autonomy within the context of shared understanding renders the chain of command unnecessary because shared understanding is highly effective in defining the boundaries in which individuals and teams can make intelligent, autonomous decisions. These boundaries are broad enough that the vast majority of operating decisions can be made by those closest to the performance of the work. Equally important, shared understanding also defines which decisions are outside the boundaries of operating teams. At Gore, this boundary is known as the waterline—a metaphor from the boating world informing a clear guidance for approaching high-risk decisions.[8] If there is a hole in the side of a boat above the waterline, there is little danger of sinking. While a repair is advisable as soon as possible, the boat can keep sailing. However, a hole below the waterline is dangerous and will probably sink the boat. Using this metaphor, if an individual or team at Gore is contemplating a decision that could cause serious damage to the enterprise, the proposed action is considered below the waterline, and individuals will use what Gore calls the Advice Process to guide decision-making in this instance.[9]

Before making a high-risk decision, advocates of an idea seek out advice from other associates who have experience related to the proposed action or who will be affected by the decision. The Advice Process is a way to expand the collective intelligence guiding the decision, and this guidance can take various forms. For example, the advice may provide insight into key considerations that could uncover critical unknown unknowns that need to be identified and handled to increase the probability of success, or it might shed light on unconscious biases that need to be set aside before crafting a credible market strategy. The advice may build on the proposed idea in a way that greatly diminishes any risk, creating an opportunity for significant growth. Finally, the advice may provide information that convinces the authors of an idea to abandon a project before investing substantial resources that they realize, with a new understanding, has no chance of succeeding. In any event, the Advice Process is a tangible example of what decision-making looks like when management focuses on expanding consciousness rather than control.

Morning Star's approach to decision-making is similarly based on the premise that all individuals have a voice in matters that affect them. Unless team members have agreed to alternative decision-making rules in advance, colleagues generally apply an approach similar to Gore's Advice Process. By bringing together all involved and giving everyone an equal voice, Morning Star can aggregate and leverage the group's collective wisdom to make highly informed decisions. Because individuals can't use coercive power to influence or dominate the group's thinking, the team can better combine the strengths of multiple perspectives to identify well-thought-out solutions that reflect a higher level of intelligence than any one person could devise. Team members are free to negotiate the ownership of decision-making rights in advance based on expertise and integrity. Decision rights are earned through trust, respect, communication, and competence. They are not entitlements handed out by managers in a hierarchy. This open approach to strategic decision-making has enabled Morning

Star to grow from a start-up to the world's largest tomato processor over the past three decades.

The primary vehicle for making operating decisions in Morning Star is the Colleague Letter of Understanding, which we discussed in Chapter 4. Once a year, as colleagues formulate their specific agreements for handling various aspects of their operations, individuals will volunteer to act as owners of a particular process, such as canning tomatoes. If one or more individuals step forward to take responsibility for a process and those involved agree, these individuals are owners or co-owners and are invested by the relevant teams with the decision rights for that process. They retain these rights as long as they make good decisions and their ownership of decisions is unchallenged. Team members are also free to negotiate service-level agreements with each other.

Individuals on teams can challenge a decision owner if they feel the approach is wrong or if a better decision is required. In that case, the challenging individual and the owner engage in a dialogue to see if they can reach an agreement. If they can, the issue is resolved. If they can't, they expand the dialogue by mutually agreeing to bring another person into the discussion to add a fresh perspective that might serve as a catalyst for arriving at a mutually acceptable solution. If expanding the participants in the dialogue is unsuccessful, as a last resort, the original two persons involved in the difference of opinion can agree to identify a knowledgeable individual to hear their perspectives and make a decision that both will agree to accept. This process is called Gaining Agreement, and it can be used to resolve any conceivable difference of opinion between colleagues in an ecosystem where everyone has an equal voice.

ENDING CORRUPTION

When Lord Acton observed that power corrupts and absolute power corrupts absolutely, the only form of social organization he knew was the centralized top-down hierarchy. His observation is important because it points out that corruption is an inherent flaw that plagues command-and-control organizations. When an elite few are endowed with unilateral decision-making authority and the legitimate exercise of coercive power, it is not surprising that many, if not most, organizational leaders will use that authority and power, either consciously or unconsciously, to advance their personal interests. Some might say it's human nature. But is it? Is it humans who are corrupt, or is it a system that enables and rewards corruption? Just because a system brings out the worst in us doesn't mean the worst is our natural condition.

As mentioned previously, who decides is the most important question that needs to be addressed when designing an organization. The answer determines what kind of system will be built, how power works, and what kind of people will be attracted to work in the organization. If the answer is the elite few, it is highly likely the organization will attract narcissistic leaders who are naturally addicted to the coercive power that is inherent in hierarchies. Their need to control others is not only realized but also legitimized, and it is this legitimized control that often fuels corruption as narcissists exploit organizations to advance their personal interests, sometimes at the company's expense. Because narcissists are incapable of empathy, they cannot connect with the human missions of organizations. Despite rhetoric about how they value their employees and customers, their words are often empty platitudes, as their actions clearly demonstrate they value money over people. Therefore, they are preoccupied with profits and often see no difference between good and bad profits. Good profits are the rewards markets pay businesses when they delight their customers with outstanding goods, services, or experiences. Bad profits are those made at the customers' expense, such as the late fees that constituted the bulk of Blockbuster's earnings.

On the other hand, if the answer to the question of who decides is everyone on the team, the collegial members of organizations will appreciate that leadership is a team activity where collaboration rather than coercion is the behavioral dynamic that defines the social interactions of the group. Accordingly, teams will likely leverage their collective intelligence to identify and execute smarter decisions by combining the strengths of different perspectives into holistic solutions to an ever-increasing number of complex issues. This collective intelligence is the foundation for the shared understanding that precludes the need for coercive control and provides the expanded consciousness that guides the alignment of distributed activities across both teams and the organization. Perhaps, most importantly, the energy that emerges from synergistic power allows self-managed teams to be far more agile in responding to rapidly changing circumstances and far more capable of innovating as new technologies transform established markets.

The essential lesson we learn from self-managed networks is that when we understand nobody is smarter than everybody, we can create organizations immune from corruption because no individual can exploit the system by advancing his or her needs to the detriment of the group. That's because in self-managed networks, no one is powerless, and no one's voice can be canceled. When everyone is powerful, and everyone's voice matters, corruption is extremely difficult, if not impossible, because individuals cannot use force to advance an unfair advantage.

Although the narcissists who tend to lead traditional hierarchies may be prone to corruption, corruption is not a natural characteristic of most people in organizations. While narcissists are addicted to control and crave power over people, the vast majority of people in organizations desire autonomy and prefer to engage in power with others. Most people are not corrupt; they work in systems designed for corruption because they endow an elite few with the authority to exercise coercive power, and it is coercive power that corrupts. The important lesson learned from my collegiate experience in building a successful simulated society and the work experiences of Gore, Morning Star, and Buurtzorg is that when an organization is designed to amplify power with people rather than power over people, the energy that is the natural byproduct of synergistic power doesn't corrupt; it enhances the human experience of its colleagues and customers.

8

DOING THE RIGHT THINGS RIGHT

While the Digital Age has begun to reshape management principles and dramatically change the work we do and how we work, business leaders' core accountabilities remain unchanged. Whether the practice of management is organized as a top-down hierarchy or a peer-to-peer network, business leaders have the same two timeless accountabilities: strategy and execution. However, how companies approach and carry out these two essential leadership tasks will change.

Historically, planning and operations have been handled as distinct activities requiring different core competencies. Planners are seen as the "big sky, out-of-the-box" thinkers who move the business forward, while the operators are valued as the "down-to-earth" pragmatists who get things done. Unfortunately, one of the consequences of this functional segregation is that middle managers and workers in top-down hierarchies usually have little understanding of the connections between these two essential business dimensions. As a result, many managers and workers are not conversant in strategic thinking and view business execution through the limited lens of performing their assigned tasks.

The most important thing to understand about strategy and execution in fast-changing times is that they are not separate activities but interrelated and interdependent responsibilities. Segregating these two core accountabilities is a serious error. In today's markets, organizing effectively means a company's management structure must foster and facilitate continual iteration between strategy and execution. Unlike in the Industrial Age, these accountabilities are not sequential events where strategy precedes execution. In the Digital Age, strategy shapes execution, and execution, in turn, molds strategy. This is why Peter Senge's vision of learning organizations is so important.

When new technologies can reshape markets in a matter of months, learning must be built into the day-to-day fabric of organizational life. This enables companies to effectively integrate new knowledge about strategic necessities into the execution process and innovations in execution into strategic direction—all in real-time. If companies are to successfully evolve from top-down hierarchies to peer-to-peer networks, they need to become much more competent in understanding the fundamentals of these two accountabilities and how they work differently in the Digital Age organization.

STRATEGY

Strategy is about *doing the right thing* by creating a service or product that delivers what's most important to customers. Having the capacity to deliver is not enough if the product or service fails to meet customers' expectations. While Blockbuster was the market leader in video rentals and Kodak excelled at film photography, these mighty companies fell because they couldn't strategically adapt to a digital world. They would each fatally discover that there is nothing more useless than doing the wrong thing right. If you want to know what's the right thing, you need to listen closely to your customers and understand what's most important to them. Few companies have done this better than Southwest Airlines, despite the difficulties of competing in a uniquely challenged industry.

Much of Southwest's longstanding success can be attributed to its clear focus on its chosen customer, the leisure traveler. With its competitors riveted to the demands of the business road warriors, Southwest saw an opportunity to deliver value to an untapped market segment with a very different set of needs and expectations.

For business travelers, timeliness and comfort are most important. With the many demands on their time, frequent fliers require flight schedules that align with their business meeting arrangements. They want to carry on their luggage, and they need to be able to quickly move on and off the aircraft so they can spend more time doing business and less time sitting on planes. While in flight, business travelers want a reserved, comfortable aisle or window seat, preferably with no one in the middle seat, so they can work more comfortably because, for road warriors, their cushion on the plane is an extension of the office. This is why frequent fliers on the major airlines board and depart first and have the most comfortable seats at the front of the plane. Another important value for business travelers is to receive timely and comfortable service at a reasonable price to keep their corporate finance departments happy at the office. Thus, the key value proposition for business travelers can be summed up as timely and comfortable service at a reasonable price.

For leisure travelers, on the other hand, low prices are most important, followed by the reliability and freedom to travel to distant places by plane rather than car. Leisure travelers don't mind checking luggage as long as they do not have to pay extra fees. They don't need assigned seats and aren't worried about working on airplanes. They're delighted to go places without having a long drive in a car and without spending more money than it would cost to drive. Leisure travelers want the reliable freedom to travel at an affordable price.

Southwest's strategic challenge was to find a way to align its core business infrastructure with a market segment where affordability was everything. The air carrier met this challenge by building its well-known low-cost business model. Southwest's fleet uses only one type of aircraft, the Boeing 737. This reduces maintenance and training costs and means that its planes are interchangeable for greater operational flexibility. Recognizing that seating preferences were not essential values for leisure travelers, Southwest could trim its technology costs by using a system of three seating groups, the now familiar A, B, and C lines.

Furthermore, by leveraging its no-frills approach, the air carrier dramatically reduced its gate turnaround time to an unprecedented twenty minutes, shattering the industry norm. Getting planes quickly back into the air generated more revenue miles per hour than their competitors, which allowed Southwest to charge lower fares and remain profitable. Finally, while other carriers have resorted to charging baggage fees to meet their cost challenges, Southwest can leverage its low-cost model to meet a very important value of the leisure traveler: no baggage fees.

By building its core business infrastructure around the most important values of its chosen customers, Southwest was able to find a way for the cost of air travel to compete favorably with the cost of driving. In meeting this challenge, they aligned strategy and execution to deliver their well-known company promise, "You are now free to move about the country." And that's exactly what millions of leisure travelers do every year.

EXECUTION

Execution is *doing things right*. It is the design and management of business processes that meet or exceed customer expectations. Like strategy, execution is riveted on delivering what's most important to customers. Where strategy is about the focus of the company's promise, execution is about the fulfillment of that promise. For example, FedEx's pledge of "absolutely, positively overnight" would be meaningless without the consistent follow-through to deliver every package the next morning. While strategy gives purpose to execution, execution gives meaning to strategy. Flawless execution lets the customer know that a company means what it promises.

The key to execution excellence is having well-designed business processes that effectively integrate the complete set of activities necessary for customers to receive the promised value every time. The prerequisites for these processes in self-managed networks are clarity—which is the bridge between strategy and execution—and voluntarism. Clarity comes from building a shared understanding of the sequence and interrelationships of activities necessary to deliver customer value and then identifying which activities are the key drivers of success. These key drivers are regularly measured in a compelling and visibly evident scorecard that tells workers how well their execution meets customers' expectations. Clarity around what we are doing and how our work together contributes to what customers value is a vital driver of execution excellence.

The late Intel CEO Andy Grove often said, "You can't manage what you don't measure."[1] Measurement is one of the most important tools for providing clarity because key metrics let people know first-hand whether they are winning or losing. In the traditional organization, managers are responsible for the design and review of key business measures. In contrast, staff are usually assigned metrics that gauge how well they carry out their designated tasks. While hierarchical managers may have a sense of the organization's overall performance, the first-hand knowledge of staff is usually restricted to how well they are doing their part of the business. In most top-down organizations, staff depend on managers to let them know how the overall business is performing.

Because self-managed organizations don't have bosses, everyone needs sufficient information to know whether the organization is winning or losing. In peer-to-peer networks, well-designed measures are essential information tools for fostering high levels of transparency, engagement, accountability, alignment, and performance. A comprehensive set of simple, relevant, and understandable measures lets everyone know what's working and what's not working. These measures enable effective self-management because when the data shows the organization is not accomplishing its goals, people figure out a way to get back on track. Colleagues in self-managed networks typically make corrections smarter and faster than their hierarchical counterparts because they are closer to the problems, better able to leverage their collective knowledge, and can initiate immediate action when they reach an agreement on what to do.

Measuring What's Most Important

An effective measurement practice should clearly spotlight the critical few actions that drive the organization's success. In choosing which actions to measure, colleagues need to take time to first understand and then measure, avoiding the bravado of setting premature goals based on impulse. While it may appear decisive, bravado is often nothing more than bold action without understanding. Often, acting without thinking causes team members to target what's easy rather than important to measure.

Key metrics should include a balance of leading and lagging indicators. This is a departure from the usual practice of traditional companies whose measurement focus is preoccupied with their lagging indicators. These performance measures provide information about outcomes and are usually easy measures to identify. These numbers are typically found in financial statements and reflect what's most important to Wall Street analysts, whose focus tends to prioritize the short term over the long term. The problem with lagging indicators is that the information provided by these measures is not actionable. If the quarterly earnings are below expectations, there's nothing anyone can do to change the result. W. Edwards Demming, the management and quality guru, cautioned against an overreliance on financial data when he pointed out that using lagging indicators as primary management tools is like "driving a car by looking in the rearview mirror."[2]

Lagging measures don't provide the most important information needed for managing businesses, especially in fast-changing times. A simple yet pervasively misunderstood rule of business is you can't manage results by tracking results. You can only manage results by tracking *the drivers of results*. This is not to imply that results are not important. Quite the contrary, achieving positive outcomes is the goal of business, and a results-oriented organization should continue to reward its members based on their performance. However, if people want to influence their results, they must focus on the critical few performance drivers. These are a company's leading indicators.

Identifying leading indicators is not as easy as it may appear because the most important drivers of performance are not always intuitively obvious. The most important lead measures are often hiding in plain sight. Still, nobody is tracking them because they are either difficult to measure or no one has made the connection between these overlooked metrics and performance.

Given the latent nature of leading indicators, team brainstorming is often the best approach to discovering these important measures. The team should be encouraged to identify as many ideas as possible and expand their thinking because lead measures can sometimes be counterintuitive. For example, in identifying its leading indicators, one company discovered that its number of days of receivables was the most informative lead indicator of customer satisfaction. They noticed that when customers were unhappy, they slowed down their payments to the company. They discovered that the receivables number was not just an accounting measure but, more importantly, an indicator of customer satisfaction. Tracking this measure became an early warning signal to let the company know when they needed to talk to their customers to rectify any issues before those customers might consider taking their business to a competitor.

A good leading indicator has two basic attributes: It's reliably predictive of achieving desired results, and it is actionable by the team members.[3] Leading indicators help colleagues know if their expected results are likely to occur. More importantly, if it appears the business is underperforming, leading indicators provide colleagues with sufficient time to decide between two very different courses of action: Do they correct or adapt?

Because traditional organizations typically use lagging indicators as their primary metrics tool, they are naturally biased to take corrective action when the numbers are poor. However, if adaptive action is what's needed to solve the problem, taking corrective action can result in managers doing the wrong thing right. Preoccupation with quarterly financial results can cause managers to miss signals that indicate the need for major change to maintain future profits. This happened when Blockbuster ignored Michael Schrage's recommendation, as discussed in Chapter 2, to discontinue its late fees and explore new ways to fulfill its mission of providing excellent home entertainment options. The video rental executives were not interested in engaging in adaptive action by exploring new ways to connect with their best—but very dissatisfied—customers. Instead, they reminded Schrage that he was hired to devise the corrective action needed to convince customers that late fees were a good value for providing flexibility for extended viewing. If Blockbuster's executives had treated customer satisfaction as a serious leading indicator, more likely than not, they would have recognized that doing the right things right meant it was Blockbuster and not the customers who needed to change.

Another important distinction between leading and lagging indicators is that while negative lagging indicators are evidence of poor performance, negative leading indicators, if handled properly, can be tools for enabling high performance. When lagging indicators are negative, the typical reaction of traditional managers is to deny, downplay, or dismiss the numbers because they are concerned the unwelcome metrics will reflect badly in their annual performance evaluations. With this mindset, negative numbers are always viewed as enemies and never as friends. Managers will likely miss opportunities to nip problems in the bud if this thinking is applied to leading indicators. When team members appreciate that negative leading indicators are friends who warn that something is wrong, they understand these metrics provide them with the timely information they need to choose between corrective or adaptive action before a small problem grows into a major crisis.

In identifying key leading indicators, less is more. The challenge is identifying the small number of measures that are the best gauges of future performance. These numbers need to be clear, and it often helps if they are color coded. Simplicity is the norm in selecting leading indicators.

When we engaged in brainstorming the signals of our future performance at Blue Cross Blue Shield FEP, we identified four lead measures that were clear drivers of either market share or profitability.

These leading indicators were measured frequently and widely broadcast in color coding so that people could see how well we performed. If these measures were positive—colored coded either blue for excellent or green for good—we could be reasonably certain that the ultimate outcomes would be positive. Conversely, if these parameters turned negative—yellow for fair or red for failing—we had a learning tool that enabled us to proactively assess our processes and environment. This approach helped us determine whether we needed to make operational or strategic adjustments in sufficient time to minimize the effects of adverse developments on our business outcomes. More importantly, we had a clear focus on the self-organization of the efforts of the thousands of individuals among the thirty-nine Blue Cross Blue Shield organizations participating in the FEP business alliance.

Discovering and building a shared understanding around the critical few drivers of success helped us focus on the right things and guided us in doing things right. When people can clearly see for themselves whether they are winning or losing, they can make the connections between their tasks and the critical drivers to self-organize their work in real time.

Recognizing Workers As Volunteers

The second prerequisite for effective execution is voluntarism. If workers are truly partners, then workers are volunteers—paid volunteers—yet volunteers all the same. Today, few, if any, employees spend their entire careers with one company. Workers remain with an organization as long as the business relationship meets their needs. If workers feel their working arrangements no longer suit them, they are likely to move to another company for as long as the next situation fulfills their needs. With the recent rapid shift in pensions from defined benefit to defined contribution, the increased portability of health insurance, and opportunities for remote working, companies have less leverage to keep workers in their employ. Today, workers have more choices about where and with whom they will work.

There was a time when the bosses could take the workers for granted and act as if their employees were assets they owned. Workers have been called "human resources" as if they were available tools along with other fixed assets such as capital resources, facilities, and equipment. Traditional corporate language and structures reflect this attitude of ownership and control, reinforcing the internalization of the notion that workers have limited voice and are hired to serve as a resource at the discretion of the managers.

In self-managed networks, workers are partners. The gardeners who lead these enterprises understand they need workers to willingly and voluntarily work for them if they want to achieve extraordinary performance. They can't afford to treat workers as subordinates or human resources. They need to see them as key contributors. In an interview, Peter Drucker captured this new reality by stating, "Today the corporation needs them [knowledge workers] more than they need the corporation. That balance has shifted."[4]

Acknowledging that workers are no longer subordinates is a dramatic shift in how companies view their employees. Being a volunteer means the workers have the right to challenge their leaders. In a true partnership, one partner cannot command or control the others. Partners collaborate, respecting each other's right to object and working on issues until a consensus is reached. While more companies are calling their employees "associates" in recognition of changing realities, the true test for whether a company is serious or just paying lip service is whether its leaders honor their workers' voices until mutual agreement is reached.

HONORING EVERYONE'S VOICE

In self-managed networks, mutual agreement is often the key to doing the right things right. Honoring the voices of everyone on a team to work through challenges and reach mutual agreement is usually the fastest path to aligning strategy and execution. I experienced this first-hand when I facilitated a collective intelligence workshop to organize action on a critical strategic initiative during my time with Blue Cross Blue Shield FEP.

By way of background, the workshop's objective was to design a new health insurance product to replace one of the two options FEP offered in the U.S. Government's Federal Employees Health Benefits Program (FEHBP). In this program, federal employees nationwide choose their health insurance from product options offered by over 250 national and local offerings. Blue Cross Blue Shield was the most popular carrier, with 49 percent of the market share at that time. Over the preceding fifteen years, Blue Cross Blue Shield had steadily increased its market share by ten percentage points on the strength of a then-new PPO (Participating Provider Option) product that, over that time, had grown to become the carrier's flagship product.

In designing and executing a new product to replace the unpopular and financially challenged second product offering, our job was to create a new option that would be more attractive to customers without diminishing the appeal of FEP's flagship product. The new offering was to be part of a growth strategy to expand into segments of the federal employee market where Blue Cross Blue Shield had historically been weak.

Based on a market segmentation analysis that had been shared with the workshop participants, it was clear that the best product design to meet this challenge was to build a lower-priced EPO (Exclusive Provider Option) offering. This would be a completely different insurance model from the flagship product as well as from the offering it was replacing, which was also a PPO product. While the proposed EPO model would provide generous benefits for using doctors and hospitals in the carrier's network, there would be no out-of-network benefits in exchange for its lower price. This meant that if someone were to use the services of a doctor or a hospital that was not part of the Blue Cross Blue Shield EPO network, the customer would be responsible for 100 percent of the costs. On the other hand, the flagship PPO product would continue to have both in-network and out-of-network benefits, with lower cost-sharing for customers who used the carrier's network of participating doctors and hospitals.

There were two major challenges to the successful execution of this strategy. First, Blue Cross Blue Shield was not certain that the Office of Personnel Management (OPM)—the agency responsible for administering health insurance benefits for federal employees—would agree to an EPO product option. Second, the execution of this new product model would require significant time-challenged modifications to the carrier's claims processing systems that would need to begin well before the annual date that Blue Cross Blue Shield and OPM normally agreed on product options for the next calendar year.

Given these two challenges and knowing that continuing with the current unpopular second product was not an option, I instructed the forty workshop participants to meet in small group discussions to identify alternative product designs in the event that OPM would not accept an EPO product. I explained that, by having an alternative, we could begin systems work on both designs until product discussions were concluded, enabling us to complete the systems installation of whichever product alternative was ultimately accepted by OPM. It sounded like a reasonable business plan, given that the board had already decided that the current second product was unsustainable and had to be replaced immediately in the next benefit year. Being prepared with alternative options would allow us to be able to handle any outcome from the product negotiations with OPM while meeting the board's requirement to install a new second product.

As was my usual practice at the start of small group discussions, I asked the participants if they had any questions before beginning the exercise. One individual from the information systems discipline spoke up and said, "I understand the exercise and what you're asking us to do, but we can't do this. It's the wrong thing to do." He went on to explain that there was no alternative to the EPO model for the new second product if we were serious about the new offering promoting a growth strategy. He asserted that we needed to commit to the EPO model and do whatever was necessary to make it happen, even if it meant waiting an additional year to get OPM comfortable with this new product design. He further stated that the existing resources could not support working on two alternative product designs concurrently. Therefore, we could not reasonably expect to do either one before the start of the next benefit year at the level necessary to deliver the expected excellent service. He reiterated that a commitment needed to be made to the EPO product and that the group should not waste any time on alternative models.

I responded to the participant by acknowledging the importance of doing everything possible to make the EPO model happen. I affirmed the difficult challenge of beginning systems work on both alternatives at once. Nevertheless, I emphasized the importance of identifying a backup alternative given the established annual schedule for product negotiations and the board's expectation for a new second product in the next benefit year. I then begged the group's indulgence and asked the participants to begin the small group discussions. Once again, the same participant raised his hand and said, "With all due respect, I have to continue to push back. We will be wasting our time; it's just the wrong thing to do if we want our new product to be a growth opportunity." This time, I noticed nods of agreement among the other participants and realized that the speaker was, in effect, an agent for the group.

There was an air of suspense in the room, as everyone knew we were in uncharted waters. While I was quite experienced at facilitating collective intelligence workshops, I had never been faced with participants refusing to participate in a small group exercise. As I looked around the room, I realized that all eyes were on me to see how I would handle this moment and to find out whether our commitment to a consensus agreement was genuine or just another example of empty rhetoric about employee involvement. It was moment-of-truth time.

I was very uncomfortable and felt under enormous pressure. On the one hand, the board wanted a new product now. On the other hand, the workshop participants were insisting that there was only one new product model that fit the strategy, even if it meant waiting a year to make it happen. I was also aware that this was an integrity moment for the collective intelligence workshop process that would impact our commitment to collaboration far beyond this session. With all this in mind, I asked the participants a third time if they would indulge me and go into the small group exercise, and for a third time, the same participant respectfully pushed back with even more nodding agreement on the part of the participants. It was then that I realized something important was happening in the room, and I needed to stop fighting it.

So, I asked the group, "What do others think?" One by one, several other participants voiced their agreement that a commitment had to be made to the EPO product model and that it would be counterproductive to work on any other alternative. Acknowledging the clear will of the group, I smiled and said, "Well, I guess we won't be doing this small group exercise this morning." Instead, I opened a discussion, sharing with the group the pressures I felt to find a solution that acknowledged the wisdom of the workshop participants while complying with the will of the board.

Over the next hour, a genuine dialogue developed as we worked on resolving these seemingly irreconcilable positions together. As the discussion evolved and the participants built upon one another's comments and observations, a breakthrough emerged as one member suggested that we accelerate the date for reaching an agreement with OPM on the form of the new product option, letting the premium rate negotiation happen later in the year at the usual time. If this could be done, the new product design would be known before beginning critical systems work, and the board's directive would be met. The creative energies of the participants then moved to outline the compelling presentation needed to convince OPM to accept an earlier date for closure on the second product model. At the end of this large group discussion, we were all very comfortable that we had created the tools to secure OPM's agreement to an earlier product closure date and, more importantly, to fully execute the systems requirements for the operational excellence our customers expected. In the end, both of these actions were successfully achieved, and the new second product exceeded the strategic growth expectations to the delight of the board and staff alike.

As a final note on this workshop experience, after the participants had concluded their work in the large group discussion, the individual continually pushing back against the small group exercise raised his hand one more time, and I remember thinking, *What now?* However, he looked at me and said, "Before we move on, I'd like to thank you for allowing us to push back and for your patience. I know this wasn't comfortable for you. We all agree that, over the last hour, we did some really fine work and landed in the right place. We wouldn't have gotten here if you hadn't allowed it. Thanks for not shutting us down." At that point, all the participants broke into spontaneous applause. Clearly, I was looking at forty very enthusiastic and committed volunteers who would ensure we did the right things right.

The clarity of the shared understanding around building the EPO product and the willingness to approach the workshop participants as volunteers were the keys to successfully designing and delivering an innovative health insurance product that exceeded customers' expectations.

A Bias for Results

As mentioned previously, the three fundamental dimensions of organizations are intelligence, power, and performance. Intelligence is the ability to solve problems, power is the capacity to take action, and performance is the wherewithal to accomplish results. Intelligence is the domain for strategy, and power is the domain for execution. The alignment of these two dimensions is the domain of performance. When top-down hierarchies leverage the intelligence of the elite few to do strategic planning and use coercive power to direct action, they tend to forecast the status quo into the future. In rapidly changing times, this can lead companies to do the wrong thing right or, worse yet, the wrong thing wrong. In either event, these organizations will struggle with performance.

On the other hand, by leveraging collective intelligence as a tool for strategic discovery and relying upon synergistic power to define action, peer-to-peer networks provide themselves with the wherewithal to change as fast as the world around them. This increases their ability to achieve extraordinary performance because by increasing their conscious competence to uncover critical blind spots, they are more likely to do the right things right.

One critical blind spot that plagues the leaders of hierarchical organizations is their bias for action. They often pride themselves on being action oriented. While they tend to perceive this action orientation as a virtue, it is often a flaw—sometimes a tragic flaw if they are doing the wrong things. Command-and-control managers often confuse action with progress, but far too often, their action orientation is nothing more than a mask for a continual pattern of crisis management. When leaders assume they have the answers, ignore those who raise questions, and go straight to action, the results are often wrought with the problems typical of a ready-fire-aim management approach that poorly utilizes scarce resources and drains the morale of the staff.

By contrast, the participants in peer-to-peer networks are more likely to be results oriented. By focusing on what's most important to customers, they understand that results, not activities, delight customers. Being quick to action diminishes the short-term anxieties of bosses. Being quick to results meets customers' needs and helps turn them into long-term purchasers. Results-oriented leaders understand the key to extraordinary performance is recognizing they don't have to have all the answers themselves because, when it comes to strategy, their primary job has much more to do with *making discoveries* than making plans.

Strategic discovery, in contrast to strategic planning, mines the collective intelligence of the whole organization to develop strategy. While decisions below the waterline—using W. L. Gore's language—may be the ultimate responsibility of a senior leadership team, self-managed networks have routine processes to provide decision-makers with information gathered from a broad spectrum of members within the organization. Accordingly, the results-oriented leaders of networks are highly skilled facilitators who excel at building consensus and shared understanding among many people. Shared understanding is the great enabler of effective decision-making and high performance because it assures that organizations are doing the right things right.

Transparency

Another benefit of shared understanding is that the resulting synergistic power created by teams enables a higher level of organizational control than compliance with the commands of controlling bosses. That's because the degree of transparency needed to build an effective shared understanding provides self-managed organizations with a much more effective control system than is ever possible in bureaucratic hierarchies.

Transparency is the most effective control system because when everyone knows everything, there are no secrets. Companies with high levels of freedom of information and action have more resources available to ensure that the business remains under control. As a result, problems don't fester, innovation is not muted, and quality is continually improved. The level of transparency needed to make self-management work eliminates the hidden agendas and the institutional ignorance that plagues organizations when secrets prevail.

Traditional hierarchical organizations have lots of secrets. With work subdivided among departments and directed by managers who are often engaged in some form of "turf battle," it is unsurprising that information does not flow freely and that many workers are unaware of what people do outside their departments. Sometimes, the secrets are intentional, such as when information is shared on a need-to-know basis or even deliberately withheld. More often than not, most corporate secrets are the unintentional consequences of the functional fragmentation of work. Whatever the reason, hierarchical organizations breed secrets, and that explains why they need elaborate control systems.

When secrets prevail, there is little or no shared understanding among the managers and workers to guide the consistent delivery of customer value. Worse yet, without the transparency that naturally accompanies shared understanding, greedy or malicious employees have plenty of opportunities to defraud the company. To protect themselves from the potential adverse consequences of bureaucratic secrets, hierarchical organizations promulgate a continuous stream of rules and regulations and establish complex control structures based on checks and balances. These structures rely upon armies of supervisors and auditors to ensure that everyone is following the rules and that people are not using their secrets to inappropriately enrich themselves. The theory is if people have someone to watch over them, the risks associated with the inevitable secrets in bureaucracies will be mitigated, and the business will be under control. However, the unfortunate irony is the application of complex rules and regulations tends to slow things down, create confusion, and weaken control.

In self-managed networks, transparency is natural. That's because the collaboration structures essential for horizontal business arrangements organically engender high-order transparency based on trust and freedom of information. People working in peer-to-peer networks have full access to financial data, business plans, market analyses, and operational metrics. Most importantly, they can independently verify this information. Stephen M. R. Covey, in *The Speed of Trust*, makes the point that transparency is "about being real and genuine and telling the truth in a way that people can verify."[5]

When companies benefit from high-order transparency, business leaders do not have to depend upon the representations of supervisors or auditors to ensure the business is running smoothly. They can take comfort in the fact that when everyone has access to everything if there's something they need to know, they will find out sooner rather than later because when everything is available to everybody, there are no secrets.

The Future of Management

A hundred years from now, when economists, sociologists, and historians recap our progress throughout the twenty-first century, two major influences they are likely to cite are the rapid proliferation of the Internet and the extraordinary growth in our knowledge of networks. These learned scholars will probably reference how a steady stream of innovative digital technologies revolutionized global commerce at the start of the century by creating unprecedented capacities for businesses to quickly access collective intelligence, facilitate expeditious organizational learning, and build an effective, shared understanding among large numbers of geographically dispersed workers. They will likely enumerate how mass collaboration reshaped every social institution as the world was rapidly transformed into both a virtual and physical global village. These scholars will also highlight how breakthrough advances in the developing network sciences spawned a dramatic revolution in the assumptions and design principles for building more highly evolved social organizations that are more human and effective.

For the last 150 years, the machine mindset has assumed a socio-economic world that follows the laws and principles of reductionistic science. Because the primary task of the Industrial Age business has been to leverage machines and maintain stability, the mechanistic paradigm of classical physics worked. However, as we continue our transition into the radically different world of the Digital Age, business leaders need to come to terms with the new reality that the mechanistic assumptions of an outdated mindset no longer fit the more complex challenges of a rapidly changing world. They need to think differently and recognize the world is not a machine; it is a complex adaptive system where the essential attribute that separates the winners and losers is the ability to adapt to rapid change. Thinking differently means embracing a new organizational paradigm that resembles a complex adaptive system, which is best accomplished by designing organizations as self-managed, peer-to-peer networks.

Melanie Mitchell, the author of *Complexity: A Guided Tour*, defines a complex adaptive system as "a system in which large networks of components with no central control and simple rules of operation give rise to complex collective behavior, sophisticated information processing, and adaptation via learning or evolution."[6] This is also a good definition of a self-managed, peer-to-peer network.

Self-managed, peer-to-peer networks are the future of management because they are better suited for solving the problems of an increasingly more complex world. Leveraging collective intelligence, engaging in iterative discovery, and building shared understanding by integrating the strengths of different points of view into mutually acceptable agreements is the new framework for how organizations solve problems. In the fast-changing times of the Digital Age, organizations are most efficient when large numbers of workers have the necessary tools to self-organize their work within a collaborative infrastructure. In this new world, business leaders need to leave control of the details to those who do the actual work. They need to understand that an organizational design's primary focus is no longer expanding control. It is now about the expansion of consciousness by overcoming the natural biases of System 1 thinking and the limitations of the single human brain. It's about abandoning coercive power *over* people and embracing synergistic power *with* people. There is a better and more human way for us to organize our work and our world. The choice is ours.

ENDNOTES

CHAPTER 1: A RADICALLY DIFFERENT WORLD

[1] Thomas L. Friedman, *Thank You for Being Late: An Optimist's Guide to Thriving in the Age of Accelerations* (New York: Farrar, Straus, and Giroux, 2016), 25.

[2] Gary Hamel with Bill Breen, *The Future of Management* (Boston: Harvard Business School Press, 2007), 16.

[3] Chris Anderson, *Makers: The New Industrial Revolution* (New York: Crown Business, 2012), 115-118.

[4] Gary Hamel and Michele Zanini, *Humanocracy: Creating Organizations as Amazing as the People Inside Them* (Boston: Harvard Business Review Press, 2020), 9.

[5] Aaron Dignan, *Brave New Work: Are You Ready to Reinvent Your Organization?* (New York: Portfolio/Penguin, 2019), 29.

[6] DXC Technology, "Digital Transformation Is Racing Ahead and No Industry Is Immune," *hbr.org*, July 19, 2017.

[7] Tony Saldanha, *Why Digital Transformations Fail: The Surprising Disciplines of How to Take Off and Stay Ahead* (Oakland, California: Berrett-Koehler, 2019), 4.

[8] Reid Hoffman and Chris Yeh, *Blitzscaling: The Lightning-Fast Path to Building Massively Valuable Companies* (New York: Currency, 2018), 65.

[9] Ibid.

[10] Friedman, 31.

[11] Abraham Maslow, *Eupsychian Management* (Homewood, Illinois: Richard D. Irwin, Inc., 1965), 151-152.

Chapter 2: An Idea Whose Time Has Passed

[1] Aaron Dignan, *Brave New Work: Are You Ready to Reinvent Your Organization* (New York: Portfolio/Penguin, 2019), 29.

[2] Peter F. Drucker, *Management Challenges for the 21st Century* (New York: Harper Business, 1999), 139.

[3] General Stanley McChrystal (U.S. Army, retired) with Tantum Collins, David Silverman, and Chris Fussell, *Team of Teams: Rules of Engagement for a Complex World* (New York: Portfolio/Penguin, 2015), 48.

[4] Jim Harter, "U.S. Employee Engagement Holds Steady in First Half of 2021," *gallup.com*, July 29, 2021.

[5] Michael Schrage, *The Innovator's Hypothesis: How Cheap Experiments Are Worth More Than Good Ideas* (Cambridge, Massachusetts: MIT Press, 2014), 77-78.

[6] Ibid., 78.

[7] Ibid., 80-81.

[8] Ibid., 82.

[9] "Blockbuster Inc. History," *fundinguniverse.com*, 2000.

[10] Ibid., 83.

[11] Reed Hastings and Erin Meyer, *No Rules Rules: Netflix and the Culture of Reinvention* (New York: Penguin Press, 2020), xi.

[12] Minda Zetlin, "Blockbuster Could Have Bought Netflix for $50 Million, but the CEO Thought It Was a Joke," *inc.com*, September 20, 2019.

[13] Ibid.

[14] "Market Cap History of Netflix from 2002 to 2021," *companiesmarketcap.com*.

[15] Gary Hamel, *What Matters Now: How to Win in a World of Relentless Change, Ferocious Competition, and Unstoppable Innovation* (San Francisco, California: Jossey-Bass, 2012), 183.

[16] Ibid., xi.

[17] Julie Whipple, *Crash Course: Accidents Don't Just Happen* (Portland, Oregon: Yamhill Canyon Press, 2018), 34.

[18] Gary Hamel with Bill Breen, *The Future of Management* (Boston: Harvard Business School Press, 2007), 6.

CHAPTER 3: DISCOVERING THE POWER OF NETWORKS

1   Joshua Cooper Ramo, *The Seventh Sense: Power, Fortune, and Survival in the Age of Networks* (New York: Little, Brown, and Company, 2016), 47-48.
2   James Surowiecki, *The Wisdom of Crowds: Why the Many Are Smarter than the Few and How Collective Wisdom Shapes Business, Economies, Societies, and Nations* (New York: Doubleday, 2004), xiv.
3   Ibid., xix-xx.
4   Erik H. Erikson, *Childhood and Society* (New York: W.W. Norton, 1950), 147-274.
5   Ramo, 128

CHAPTER 4: BUILDING TEAMS OF LEADERS

1   Gary Hamel, *The Future of Management* (Boston, MA: Harvard Business School Press), 2007, 16.
2   Jim Collins, *Good to Great: Why Some Companies Make the Leap...and Others Don't* (New York: HarperCollins), 2001, 6.
3   Ibid., 1.
4   Ibid., 12-13.
5   General Stanley McChrystal with Tatum Collins, David Silverman, and Chris Fussell, *Team of Teams: New Rules of Engagement for a Complex World* (New York: Portfolio/Penguin), 2015, 84.
6   Ibid., 224.
7   Ibid., 225-226.
8   Ibid., 149.
9   Ibid., 145.
10 Ibid., 149.
11 Ibid., 227.
12 Bryce G. Hoffman, *American Icon: Alan Mulally and the Fight to Save Ford Motor Company* (New York: Crown Business), 2012, 72.
13 Chris McChesney, Sean Covey, and Jim Huling, *The 4 Disciplines of Execution: Achieving Your Wildly Important Goals* (New York: Free Press), 2012, 6.
14 Ibid., 6.

[15] Bryce Hoffman, "Here's Why Ford's Mark Fields Had To Go," *Forbes. com*, posted May 22, 2017.

[16] Ibid.

[17] Ibid.

[18] Ibid.

CHAPTER 5: SELF-MANAGEMENT PIONEERS

[1] Frederic Laloux, *Reinventing Organizations: A Guide to Creating Organizations Inspired by the Next Stage of Human Consciousness* (Brussels, Belgium: Nelson Parker, 2014), 2.

[2] Ibid., 14.

[3] Ibid., 36.

[4] Ibid., 20.

[5] Ibid., 36.

[6] Ibid., 32-34.

[7] Ibid., 62.

[8] Ibid., 80.

[9] Gary Hamel with Bill Breen, *The Future of Management* (Boston: Harvard Business School Press, 2007), 87.

[10] Ibid., 89.

[11] Ibid., 88-89.

[12] Alan Deutschman, "The Fabric of Creativity," *Fast Company*, December 2004, 54.

[13] Hamel with Breen, 87.

[14] Ibid., 91.

[15] Malcolm Gladwell, *The Tipping Point: How Little Things Can Make a Big Difference* (New York: Little, Brown and Company, 2000), 186.

[16] Simon Sinek, *Leaders Eat Last: Why Some Teams Pull Together and Others Don't* (New York: Portfolio /Penguin, 2017), 143.

[17] Nicholas A. Christakis and James H. Fowler, *Connected: The Surprising Power of Our Social Networks and How They Shape Our Lives* (New York: Little, Brown and Company, 2009), 248.

[18] Gary Hamel, *What Matters Now: How to Win in a World of Relentless Change, Ferocious Competition, and Unstoppable Innovation* (San Francisco: Josey-Bass, 2012), 126.

19 Hamel with Breen, 93.

20 Deutschman, 54.

21 Laloux, 112-113.

22 Hamel, 211.

23 Ibid., 212-213.

24 Ibid., 213.

25 Ibid., 227.

26 Laloux, 63.

27 Ibid.

28 Ibid., 65.

29 Ibid.

30 Ibid., 66.

31 Gary Hamel and Michele Zanini, *Humanocracy: Creating Organizations as Amazing as the People Inside Them* (Boston: Harvard Business Review Press, 2020), xi.

32 Ibid.

33 Peter Senge, *The Fifth Discipline: The Art and Practice of the Learning Organization* (New York: Doubleday/Currency), 1990.

CHAPTER 6: AN EXTRAORDINARY LEAP IN INTELLIGENCE

1 "Market Cap History of Netflix from 2002 to 2021," *companiesmarketcap.com.*

2 Donald Rumsfeld, *Known and Unknown: A Memoir* (New York: Penguin Group), 2011, xiv.

3 Daniel Kahneman, *Thinking Fast and Slow* (New York: Farrar, Straus, and Giroux), 2011, 88.

4 Ibid., 367.

5 Ibid.

6 Ibid., 368.

7 Ibid., 369.

8 Ibid.

9 Ibid., 13.

Chapter 7: When Power Does Not Corrupt

[1] John Hagel III and John Seely Brown, "Measuring the Forces of Long-Term Change—the 2010 Shift Index," Deloitte Center for the Edge.

[2] Margaret J. Wheatley, *Leadership and the New Science: Discovering Order in a Chaotic World* (San Francisco: Berrett-Koehler Publishers, 1999), 40.

[3] Reed Hastings and Erin Meyer, *No Rules Rules: Netflix and the Culture of Reinvention* (New York: Penguin Press, 2020), 64-66.

[4] Ibid., 65.

[5] Paul P. Baard, Edward L. Deci, and Richard M. Ryan, "Intrinsic Need Satisfaction: A Motivational Basis of Performance and Well-Being in Two Work Settings," *Journal of Applied Social Psychology* 34 (2004)

[6] Frederic Laloux, *Reinventing Organizations: A Guide to Creating Organizations Inspired by the Next Stage of Human Consciousness* (Brussels, Belgium: Nelson Parker, 2014), 67.

[7] Ibid.

[8] Aaron Dignan, *Brave New Work: Are You Ready to Reinvent Your Organization?* (New York: Portfolio/Penguin, 2019), 69-70.

[9] Ibid., 70.

Chapter 8: Doing the Right Things Right

[1] Michael Wade, James Macaulay, Andy Noronha, and Joel Barbier, *Orchestrating Transformation: How to Deliver Winning Performance with a Connected Approach to Change* (Lausanne, Switzerland: International Institute for Management Development, 2019), 116.

[2] Chris McChesney, Sean Covey, and Jim Huling, *The 4 Disciplines of Execution: Achieving Your Wildly Important Goals* (New York: Free Press, 2012), 49.

[3] Ibid., 12.

[4] Elizabeth Hass Edersheim, *The Definitive Drucker* (New York: McGraw Hill, 2007), 11.

[5] Stephen. M. R. Covey, *The Speed of Trust: The One Thing That Changes Everything,* (New York: Free Press, 2006), 153.

[6] Melanie Mitchell, *Complexity: A Guided Tour,* (New York: Oxford University Press, 2009), 13

Acknowledgments

This book could never have been written without the generous support of friends, family, coworkers, colleagues, and mentors. I have had the privilege of sharing this exploration of new ways of managing with many remarkable people, some through their constant encouragement, others through our work together, a special few through long conversations, and many more through the wisdom of their written words. However our paths have crossed, they have all influenced the ideas contained in this book.

I would like to first thank the three founders of the self-management pioneers featured in this book: Bill Gore, Chris Rufer, and Jos de Blok. Their insights, creativity, and courage have given the world of work a priceless gift in the form of organizations where there are no bosses, and everyone is a leader. Without their fortitude, example, and deep confidence in their colleagues, we might never know there's a better way for people to work together.

I am particularly grateful to Doug Kirkpatrick, whose thirty-year career with Chris Rufer's Morning Star began on day one, and Michael Pacanowsky, a three-decade veteran at W.L. Gore and Associates as well as the founding director of the Center for Innovative Cultures at the Bill and Vieve Gore School of Business of Westminster College. These two management innovators graciously engaged in many hours of conversation describing their experiences working in highly effective self-managed enterprises.

I am also grateful to all my many friends and colleagues in the Blue Cross Blue Shield organizations throughout the United States for their commitment and dedication to serving the millions of customers in the Federal Employee Program. I am particularly grateful to Steve Gammarino, who provided me the platform, the freedom, and the constant support to lead a multibillion-dollar business unit where I could apply the principles and practices of self-managed peer-to-peer networks in realizing the largest five-year growth period in the sixty-year history of the business.

Many thanks to the following for investing hours in reading parts of the manuscript or discussing its underlying principles: Roger Allen, Rosemarie Barbeau, Bill Beausay, Sue Bingham, Dennis Carrai, Larry Cooper, Dawna Jones, Henri Lipmanowicz, Keith McClandless, Dan Montgomery, Jim Parker, Fred Plumb, Bill Sanders, Annie Snowbarger, Peter Stevens, and Robert White.

I am also indebted to the many intellectual pioneers whose writings have opened me to new ways of thinking about and practicing the art of management: Chris Anderson, Joel Barbier, Ori Brafman, John Seely Brown, Ram Charan, Nicholas A. Christakis, Clayton Christensen, Jim Collins, Aaron Dignan, Peter Drucker, James H. Fowler, Thomas L. Friedman, John Hagel III, Gary Hamel, Reed Hastings, Dee Hock, Bryce Hoffman, Reid Hoffman, Tony Hsieh, Daniel Kahneman, Polly La Barre, Frederic Laloux, James Macaulay, John Mackey, Abraham Maslow, General Stanley McChrystal, Melanie Mitchell, Andy Noronha, Harrison Owen, Joshua Cooper Ramo, Eric Raymond, Michael Schrage, Peter M. Senge, Simon Sinek, James Surowiecki, Michael Wade, Margaret J. Wheatley, and Michele Zanini.

I would like to express my appreciation for my agent, Sandra Bond, who, over the years, has provided invaluable assistance and support. I am grateful for the contributions of Chris O'Byrne, Debbie O'Byrne, and the editors at Jetlaunch, whose professional dedication exceeded every expectation.

Finally, I am deeply thankful for the love and support of my wife, Glenda, who found the time and energy to review the early drafts of the book, improving it immeasurably. I am also thankful for the blessing of our blended family, our four daughters Melissa, Meghan, Erin, and Emily, their spouses Bruce, David, Brian, and Trey, as well as our ten grandchildren whose joy and enthusiasm make every day a great day.

www.ingramcontent.com/pod-product-compliance
Lightning Source LLC
Chambersburg PA
CBHW021501180326
41458CB00050B/6862/J